"Waiting for the Coming"

"Waiting for the Coming of our Lord Jesus Christ."

1 Corinthians 1:7

J T Mawson

Scripture Truth Publications

"WAITING FOR THE COMING"

Revised and reprinted from a series entitled "The Coming Again of the Lord Jesus" in "Scripture Truth" magazine, Volume 25, 1933 and the article "He that shall come, will come" in Volume 26, 1934.

First published 1935 in hardback by Pickering & Inglis, Printers and Publishers, London and The Central Bible Truth Depôt, 5 Rose Street, Paternoster Square, London, E.C.4

Re-typeset with amended/additional references and transferred to Digital Printing 2011

ISBN: 978-0-901860-67-5 (paperback)

Copyright © 2011 Scripture Truth Publications

A publication of Scripture Truth

All rights reserved. No part of this publication may be reproduced, stored in a retrieval system, or transmitted, in any form or by any means, electronic, mechanical, photocopying, recording or otherwise without prior permission of Scripture Truth Publications.

Scripture quotations, unless otherwise indicated, are taken from The Authorized (King James) Version. Rights in the Authorized Version are vested in the Crown. Reproduced by permission of the Crown's patentee, Cambridge University Press.

Scripture quotations marked "N.Tr." are taken from "The Holy Scriptures, a New Translation from the Original Languages" by J. N. Darby (G Morrish, 1890)

Cover photograph ©iStockphoto.com/Ynot2 (Gilad Levy)

Published by Scripture Truth Publications
31-33 Glover Street,
Crewe, Cheshire, CW1 3LD

Scripture Truth is an imprint of Central Bible Hammond Trust, a charitable trust

We are grateful to Les Hodgett for providing text from a scan of the first edition.
Typesetting by John Rice
Printed by Lightning Source

Preface to 2011 Edition

In 1933 a series of Bible Studies appeared in *Scripture Truth* magazine with the title *The Coming Again of the Lord Jesus*. The theme was dear to the heart of its author, for in the summer of that year he addressed "a conference for the help of younger Christians" on the subject "Behold, He cometh" (Revelation 1:5-8):

> "We belong to the new era, we are children of the day. The faithful Witness has brought the light of it to us. As the First-begotten of the dead, He has imparted to us His own life; in Him we live the life that belongs to the day, and He must be our Leader, our Prince. If we yield our lives to Him, He will direct us and we shall live wisely and walk wisely, and the peace that belongs to the day will be in our hearts, and the light of the day will shine in our lives to enlighten those who are groping in the night. And meanwhile *we shall look for His coming*."

People have all sorts of ideas about what the future holds. What is *the truth* about what lies ahead? The Bible records that Jesus said He would return. Is that true? and, if so, what are the consequences—for the Christian and the world? In a series of Bible studies the author explores these and related issues: considering relevant questions, to which he discovers convincing answers. In the light of these, we each need to face the challenge, "Am I waiting for the coming of the Lord Jesus Christ?"

The text of the first edition has been re-typeset. A few spelling and quotation corrections were necessary. To assist the twenty-first century reader, minor changes in presentation have been made. The use of quotation (speech) marks has been updated. The full title of the book is provided in Scripture references to facilitate ease of lookup. Some references have been added to Scriptures quoted because not all today are as familiar with the Bible as those of J T Mawson's generation.

The publishers commend this book to you. As you read it, and look up the Bible references for yourself, may it encourage you to be actively "waiting for the coming" of the Lord Jesus Christ.

John Rice

"WAITING FOR THE COMING"

Contents

Preface to the 2011 Edition 3

Explanation 7

Will He Really Come Again? 11

"Behold the Bridegroom" 21

The Rapture and the Appearing 31

Will all Who are Christ's Be Caught Up
    at His Coming for His Saints? 41

"Surely, I Come Quickly" 49

Signs of His Coming 57

Waiting, Watching, Working 69

The Judgment Seat of Christ 77

The Judgment of the Living and the Dead 85

The Herald of His Coming 91

The Gospel of the Kingdom 99

The Word of God and the Coming of the Lord 107

Events to Take Place on Earth
    Between the Rapture and the Eternal State 113

Anticipation (poetry) 125

"WAITING FOR THE COMING"

Explanation

In these pages I have endeavoured to show that the coming again of the Lord Jesus Christ will be in two stages—the coming FOR His saints and WITH them, and in doing this I have used words that are current amongst Christians, namely, THE RAPTURE AND THE APPEARING. The latter is a Biblical word, the former is not, and it may not be a familiar word in this connection to many; for these reasons I had some hesitation in using it. But it is a convenient and effective word, and if the reader will bear in mind that wherever I have used it, it stands, not for a rapture of the mind or spirit, but for the actual catching away bodily of the saints of God to meet the Lord in the air (1 Thessalonians 4:17), what otherwise might be a difficulty will become simple.

May every reader be amongst those who are waiting for the coming of our Lord Jesus Christ. To whom be glory, both now and for ever.

J. T. Mawson

"WAITING FOR THE COMING"

Will He Really Come Again?

Will He really come again?

The scoffers are saying, "Where is the promise of His coming?" But Simon Peter prophesied of this in the year AD 66, and warned us that when they mocked our hope in this way we might know that we were in the last days.

Three reasons why He must come.

His first words as to it.

"WAITING FOR THE COMING"

Will He Really Come Again?

Will He really come again? Long has He been expected; will He fulfil that expectation? May it not be a vain hope? "Behold the Bridegroom cometh" (Matthew 25:6), was a great text with earnest men nigh upon a century ago, and the hope of His coming spread amongst those who loved His name, until many were saying: "Even so, come Lord Jesus" (Revelation 22:20). It became a theme of ordinary conversation. I heard of it as a child. It was talked about in our home, and I remember that one of the first teachers I ever had, asked me: "What do they preach in the meetings you go to?" I answered: "They preach that the Lord Jesus is coming again." "What!" she exclaimed, evidently startled. "Yes," I said, "and we believe it, because the Bible says so." It was a child's answer, but it shows that whether true or false this teaching had made a deep impression on my mind.

But that was many years ago, and He has not come yet, and those who looked for Him so earnestly in those years that are past have fallen asleep without realizing their hope. Were they deceived in their belief? And are we? Will He really come? The scoffers are saying: "Where is the promise of His coming?" and we must answer their challenge. What shall the answer be?

First Reason

Our answer is: "Yes, He will surely come", and the basis of our confidence is that He has said so. We do not build our hope on signs and portents, they may easily and often deceive us, but we rest in His own Word, for that cannot fail. He must come because He has said, "I will come again" (John 14:3).

Other prophecies have been fulfilled, and so shall this be. God declared in the Garden of Eden that the woman's Seed should bruise the Serpent's head. It was the first word that was ever uttered as to the coming of the great Deliverer, and that word was fulfilled when the due time came. Four thousand years passed between the prediction and its fulfilment, and throughout those long, long years men of faith waited and watched. They carried the torch of faith and hope in the darkness for a while, each in his own day, and then handed it on to their successors, until at last He for whom they looked appeared; the Day-star from on high visited them, and faith and hope gave place to sight as they gave thanks to God and cried, "Our eyes have seen Thy salvation."

God's prophets had spoken of the sufferings of Christ and of the glory that should follow. When He did appear His disciples thought only of the glory. But the glory was not yet to be, it awaited His Second Coming. It behoved Him first to suffer "that the Scriptures might be fulfilled." His first coming was for shame and spitting, for suffering and death; His second coming will be for honour and glory, for the crown and the throne. He told His disciples in the plainest language that He had come to suffer, that He would be delivered to the Gentiles and be mocked and crucified. It seemed much more likely that He would be stoned, indeed the Jews in their frenzied hatred of Him attempted this more than once, but they could not do it, a power they did not understand restrained them, *"that the Scripture might be fulfilled."* But why should He be crucified? This was a Roman mode of execution, and He did not come into conflict with Rome. He offered no resistance to Caesar's authority, but on the contrary He taught that what was due to him must be rendered to him, and for that saying the Jews hated Him the more, but the Romans had no cause to condemn Him for such teaching, He was no criminal according to their laws. Yet they crucified Him. Why? *Because the Scriptures had said that thus He would die,* and they cannot fail. More than one thousand years before it happened it was all foretold in the most graphic detail (Psalm 22). Long before the Roman power had any existence the very way they would treat Him was revealed, and the ancient word was fulfilled to the last letter of it. And by His own words He confirmed what was written of Him. *He said He would die, and He did,* HE SAID HE WOULD RISE THE THIRD DAY, AND HE DID, *HE SAID HE WOULD COME AGAIN* IN GLORY, *AND HE WILL.*

Every word of Scripture that foretold His first coming and His sufferings when He came has been fulfilled, and just as surely shall every word that has been spoken about His second coming in glory be fulfilled. If He does not come again His own Word and the Scripture will be broken, and this cannot be: Heaven and earth shall pass away, but not one jot or tittle of His Word can fail. Our first and greatest reason then for holding the coming again of our Lord as a sure and blessed hope is His own Word, and the Word of Holy Scripture.

Second Reason

The Divine plan and purpose will be incomplete if He does not come. If Sir Christopher Wren had built St. Paul's cathedral without its dome, we should have said that it was not finished, that the crown of it was wanting. And if the Lord Jesus does not come again there will be a great want in the ways of God. To come first in humiliation and not come again in power, to suffer and die for sin and not come again in glory to establish righteousness in the world where wickedness has so long held sway, to bear the Cross and not wear the Crown, would be to leave unfinished God's great scheme of blessing for men and glory for His Son. The crown of His purpose would be lacking, and the universe would say that God was not wise, or He had not the power to make His wisdom effectual. Yes, the once suffering Saviour must come in glory; where He was dishonoured He must be exalted; He loved righteousness and hated iniquity, therefore His throne must be established for ever. He must come again to bring to its consummation the whole will and purpose of God.

Third Reason

His love demands it. He cannot leave even the bodies of His blood-redeemed saints under the power of death. He must raise them up again, and He will do this at His coming again: then shall be brought to pass the saying that is written, "Death is swallowed up in victory" (1 Corinthians 15:54). And then will He present to Himself His Church, His Bride, without spot or wrinkle or any such thing. The patriarch Jacob would not have been satisfied to have laboured and waited for Rachel, and not have possessed her, yet love's labour might have been lost in his case, but the Lord's great sacrifice and labour of love cannot be lost. He must see of the travail of His soul and be satisfied, and this can only be when He receives to Himself His Church, all glorious, without spot or wrinkle or any such thing, and this cannot be apart from His coming again. Because His love demands it, we read: "The Lord Himself shall descend from Heaven with a shout, with the voice of the archangel and the trump of God; and the dead in Christ shall rise first; then we which are alive and remain shall be caught up together with them in the clouds, to meet the Lord in the air; and so shall we ever be with the Lord" (1 Thessalonians 4:16-17). "And then shall be heard as it were the voice of a great multitude and as the voice of many waters, and as the voice of mighty thunderings, saying, Alleluia, for the Lord God Omnipotent reigneth. Let us be glad and rejoice, and give honour to Him; for *the marriage of the Lamb is come*" (Revelation 19:6-7). He must come again for His church. His love demands it.

The first message that the ascended Lord sent from the glory to His disciples upon earth was that He would come back again (Acts 1:11), and His last message from the glory to His church on earth is, "Surely I come quickly" (Revelation 22:20). Truly His coming again lies very near to His heart.

THE FIRST MENTION OF HIS COMING FOR HIS SAINTS (JOHN 14)

I do want to stress the fact that the Lord's love for His own makes it imperative that He should come for them. He has told us that in His Father's house there are many mansions. He does not leave us in the world because there is only room for Him and none for us in the Father's house. There is room there for us all, had there not been He would have told us long ago, and not have drawn us after Him as He has done. He has won our hearts, because He wants us THERE. His disciples, to whom these words were first spoken, had looked for a place here in an earthly kingdom, He was going to prepare a place for them there, *in the Father's House.* They had looked for honour and power on earth, He had something better for them in Heaven. He had a *Home* for them there—home and love; His own home, His Father's love. This they were to share with Him, for nothing would satisfy His love but sharing it with them. And this is our prospect. The light of it shines with a soft and comforting radiance into our hearts, it fills us with longing for its realisation, for the longing to have us there is in His heart.

And He is coming for us. He will not send for us. We are too precious to Him, too dearly loved for that. He will come Himself. "I will come again and receive you unto Myself, that where I am there ye may be also" (John 14:3). Had we known Him only as a great potentate, splendid in His glory and supreme in dignity, then it would have been fitting that some noble servant should have been sent forth to lead us into His presence chamber to touch the sceptre that He might condescendingly extend to us. But it is not glory, or dignity, or splendour of that sort that is revealed to us here, but love; yearning, tender love that can neither wait until we are brought, nor send another for us, but must come itself. The first face that our eyes shall gaze upon at His Coming will be His own face. Countless hosts will attend Him, but they are not mentioned here, nor will they fill our vision then. It will be Himself, and Himself alone. And to Himself He will receive us, that where He is there we may be also.

It is the voice of our great Lover that speaks to us here in words so tender and true and wise, and His voice thrills our hearts, and to us it is enough that where He is there we shall be. Scant is our knowledge of the place; we do not know its glories, its extent, its location, nor are we concerned to know; it suffices us to know that it is the Father's house, and Christ is there, and He wants us to be there to share it with Himself, and we want to be there because He wants to have us there. These are the longings that His love has begotten in our hearts, and so we say, "Even so, come, Lord Jesus."

"WAITING FOR THE COMING"

"Behold the Bridegroom"

Early in the history of the church on earth the fact of the return of the Lord was lost.

Evil servants began to say, "My Lord delayeth His coming."

And the Church slumbered and slept.

But the midnight cry has gone forth, and many are now going forth to meet Him.

The truth misunderstood.

In this chapter we show how the hope was lost and regained.

"WAITING FOR THE COMING"

"Behold the Bridegroom"

Who can deny that the coming of the Lord Jesus Christ is one of the chief themes of the Bible? Certainly not those who study its pages. However much they may differ as to the manner and the meaning of it, they must all agree that it is kept continually in the forefront of God's communications to men. The first of all the prophets cried, "The Lord cometh with ten thousands of His saints" (Jude 1:14). And as prophets, priests and kings strayed from the right ways of God, and the world's problems became more involved, and its miseries increased, the coming of the Lord, as Deliverer and Judge, became more and more the burden of the men who spoke for God, and the hope of those who believed.

If we had only the Old Testament and not the New, we should find it difficult to understand why in one place His coming is said to be for suffering and humiliation, and in another for glory and power and world-wide dominion; how and why His visage would be more marred than any man's, and yet He be exalted and lifted up and made very high and astonish nations by the splendour of His majesty. The New Testament is the key to the Old, and by it the whole subject of the coming of the Lord is opened up for us, and we learn that two comings were in view, at the first of which the sufferings of Christ would be fulfilled, and at the second, the glories that should follow. Our position lies between the two.

HE CAME ONCE

He came once, not to be ministered unto, but to minister and to give His life a ransom for many.

Then He was wounded for our transgressions; then He died for our sins, according to the Scriptures; and was buried, and rose again the third day, according to the Scriptures. After that He showed Himself by many infallible proofs to His disciples, and ascended to Heaven in their sight. With hearts aglow with devotion to Him they gazed with wonder after Him as the cloud of glory received Him, and immediately two heavenly messengers stood at their sides and announced to them the fact that He—THIS SAME JESUS, AND NOT ANOTHER— would so come, as they had seen Him go. It was the first message from the glory after His entrance into it, and it became an integral part of the apostles' preaching—the testimony of the Lord. He had been here, and He had returned to Heaven from whence He came, but He would come back again. He would come in glory to judge the world in righteousness, and rule the nations with a rod of iron, and banish sorrow and crying from the earth, and bring in lasting gladness and wonderful peace.

Those that hearkened to the preaching and believed, "turned to God from idols, to serve the living and true God and to wait for His Son from heaven" (1 Thessalonians 1:9-10). The coming again of the Lord Jesus was a living hope and not a doctrine only to those early Christians; it affected them mightily *and they went forth to meet the Bridegroom.*

The world was well lost for them as they rejoiced in the hope of the coming glory of the Son of God, even Jesus, who had delivered them from the wrath to come.

A Slumbering Church

But while He tarried, the deep slumber, against which they were warned again and again in the epistles of Paul, overcame them, and the prophetic parable of our Lord was fulfilled, "they all slumbered and slept" (Matthew 25:5). The church became totally indifferent to the truth of the Lord's return, and all were alike in this, wise and foolish, true possessors and mere professors settled down in the world that He will judge at His coming, as though there were no difference between them and it. Their lamps burned but dimly, and the darkness steadily deepened, until was reached that period known as the Dark Ages. This was the midnight hour indeed, when the church that professed the Name of Christ, and which should have shone with a great light in the darkness to guide the feet of the people in the way of truth, robbed them of any light they might have had by its gross sensuality and apostasy from the truth.

The Dark Ages

The history of the church on earth was faithfully forecast in those solemn messages from the Lord to the seven churches in Asia (Revelation 2 and 3), and the period of this dense darkness is described in the central message of the seven, that to the church at Thyatira. In it the depths of Satan were known as nowhere else on earth. At that time popes, cardinals, priests and monks lived openly wicked lives, they turned the most sacred things into subjects for their obscene jests, they were profligate in conduct and profane in their conversation. It was a common saying: "If there is a hell, Rome is built over it: it is an abyss whence issues every kind of sin" [quoted by Martin Luther, recorded in Jean-Henri Merle d'Aubigné, *History of the Reformation of the Sixteenth Century*]. But worse than all, the people were corrupted by these ministers of Satan, and to them were sold indulgences which granted them pardon and secured them from the punishment beforehand of any crime that they wished to commit. And as the great dignitaries of the church required money in order to pursue their rascalities, the people were urged and forced to buy these indulgences or lose their immortal souls. Standards of right and wrong were obliterated, for the people could do what they pleased as long as they paid, and this was called the "richly offered grace of God". "We Italians", said a historian of that period, "are principally indebted to the church for having become impious and immoral" [Niccolò Machiavelli, *Discourses on the First Decade of Livy*].

THE MIDNIGHT CRY

It is in the message to the church of Thyatira, which describes this midnight period, that the Lord brings out afresh the fact of His coming. There were those in the midst of all its corruptions and darkness who were faithful to Him. A small remnant they probably were, but they were precious to the Lord, as were those who feared Him and talked together about Him in the days when Malachi prophesied. To these the Lord said, "I will put upon you none other burden, but that which ye have already, *hold fast till I come*" (Revelation 2:24-25). And wonderful words must those have been for those who had ears to hear during that dark period: *"I will give him the morning star"* (verse 28). In the records that have come down to us from those days we find that there were some who "trimmed their lamps", many more no doubt than we could know of, for the Lord has always had His thousands who did not bow the knee to Baal (1 Kings 19:18; Romans 11:4).

But were they many or few that heard the cry, "Behold, the Bridegroom", in this midnight hour, it is certain that the Lord then commenced in a special way to prepare a people to meet Him at His coming. He formed and fitted Luther for this purpose, and the most blessed truth of justification by faith instead of works was proclaimed and believed by many.

The consequence of being justified by faith is the sealing by the Holy Spirit. We are taught in Romans 5 that when justified by faith the love of God is shed abroad in our hearts by the Holy Spirit that is given unto us; and this is confirmed by Ephesians 1:13: "In whom (Christ) ye also trusted, after that ye heard the word of truth, the gospel of your salvation: in whom also after that ye believed, ye were sealed with that Holy Spirit of promise." Only those in whom the Spirit of God dwells are ready to meet the Bridegroom when He shall come, for the oil that the wise virgins took in their vessels is unquestionably a symbol of the Holy Spirit. He only can keep the lamps of our testimony burning during the absence of the Lord.

THE TRUTH MISUNDERSTOOD

From that time the coming of the Lord began to have, more or less, a place in the preaching of the Word. But it was not understood by the preachers, nor clearly preached, for the distinction between the church and the world was not discerned, and this great truth, along with all prophetic truth, must be obscure to all who do not see and maintain this distinction. It was thought and preached that the world would first be converted by the preaching of the Gospel, and that then the Lord would come and establish His kingdom of righteousness; and this by pious men who no doubt read and studied their Bibles. It is still a popular notion, but as false as it is popular. How it could have gained currency is difficult to understand with such a solemn passage in the Bible as that in Revelation 1:7: "Behold, He cometh with clouds; and every eye shall see Him, and they also which pierced Him: and all kindreds of the earth shall wail because of Him. Even so, Amen." A converted world would surely receive Him with acclamation and not wailing. There are many other passages which are equally emphatic, such as 2 Thessalonians 1:7-9; Revelation 6:15-17; 19:11-16. But men believe what pleases them, and the thought of the intervention of the Lord in judgment is not pleasant to those who love the world or are involved in its many schemes for its own greatness. And those who were true to their Lord misread the Word of truth because they did not rightly divide it.

After the Reformation the church soon settled down again in the world. It has been said that the ambition of the Romish church is to dominate the world; it did in former days, and will do so again, but in Protestantism the world rules the church; it certainly does in the state churches where its very doctrines are secured and fixed by act of Parliament. Hence in the message to Sardis which describes this condition of things, the Lord says, "Thou hast a name that thou livest, and art dead" (Revelation 3:1). And, *"I will come on thee as a thief"* (verse 3), which is the character in which He will come to the world, which cares nothing about His coming, except to scoff at it, or hate the thought of it; thus will He come to the unwatchful and indifferent church.

"BEHOLD THE BRIDEGROOM"

The Renewed Cry

But the cry which went forth first at the midnight of the church's history is sounding louder now, for in the message to the church at Philadelphia the Lord says, *"Behold, I come quickly:* hold fast that which thou hast, that no man take thy crown" (Revelation 3:11). And this word has awakened a response in many hearts, and these bear in some degree Philadelphian characteristics, which are, loyalty to the Word of the Lord, devotion to His name and love to all the brethren. May they greatly increase and grow for His Name's sake.

Numbers have been recovered to the truth of the Lord's coming. It has become again a real and living hope, but it is only real and living to those who have trimmed their lamps, for two things are infallibly united, devotion to Christ and witness to the world. Those who are really looking for Christ, who are truly saying, "Come, Lord Jesus", will by their very lives bear a witness to the world, they will shine as lights as they pass through it, for they will not settle down in it.

Their testimony will be that the Lord is coming, and that they are going forth to meet Him. The world's fashions and ways, and schemes and ambitions will not engage and entangle them, for they know that it lies under judgment, along with Satan, its god and prince, and that its time is short and its doom is sealed. Yet they will not be indifferent to the needs of men, they will mingle with their testimony the evangelistic cry: "Whosoever will, let him take the water of life freely" (Revelation 22:17).

This cry, "Behold, the Bridegroom", is a great test. It finds us out. It tested these awakened virgins in the prophetic parable, and we learn from it that the test is intensely individual. To what community you belong is not the test, nor what profession you make, everything depends upon whether you have the oil in your vessel—Have you received the Holy Spirit? And none can receive Him for another, or having received Him, impart Him to another. Each must receive Him for himself.

The Time is Short

The time is short. Fleeter than these foolish virgins imagined were the feet of the Bridegroom, for while they went to secure the oil for their vessels, He came, and they that were ready went in with Him to the marriage, and THE DOOR WAS SHUT. It was too late then for them to buy the oil or enter the door, and their knocking was in vain. The Bridegroom only knew those who possessed the oil, and only those whom He knew passed with Him in to the marriage feast.

Are any who read in doubt as to this vital and indispensable possession? and do they ask, Where can we buy the oil? To buy indicates a personal transaction. You must have personal dealings with God, first as to your own sinfulness and need of a Saviour, and then as to the Saviour that He has provided. Paul preached, "repentance towards God and faith in our Lord Jesus Christ" (Acts 20:21), and Peter declared, "The God of our fathers raised up Jesus, whom ye (Jews) slew and hanged on a tree. Him hath God exalted with His right hand to be a Prince and a Saviour, for to give repentance to Israel, and forgiveness of sins. And we are His witnesses of these things; and so is also THE HOLY GHOST, WHOM GOD HATH GIVEN TO THEM THAT OBEY HIM" (Acts 5:30-32).

The Rapture and the Appearing

The Lord's Second Coming will be in two parts.

In this chapter we endeavour to show the difference between the two.

The law of gravitation.

Types of the Rapture.

The spiritual body.

"WAITING FOR THE COMING"

The Rapture and the Appearing

It would not be right to say that the Coming Again of the Lord Jesus will be two comings, yet it is clear from Scripture that it will be in two stages. The first will be His coming FOR His saints: they are to be *"caught up"* to meet the Lord in the air (1 Thessalonians 4:16-17). This is spoken of as *the Rapture*. The second, His coming WITH them, is called *the Appearing*, *i.e.*, His manifestation to the world. A good text for this is, "When Christ who is our life shall appear, then shall ye also appear with Him in glory" (Colossians 3:4).

Question: *Which of these two stages of the coming ought we to preach to the world?*

The Appearing is our testimony to the world; the truth of the "catching up" does not seem to have been given for public preaching to the world, but for the comfort of the hearts of the Lord's own in the world, as we shall see; but the appearing of the Lord in glory has been the testimony of His witnesses from the beginning. Enoch, the seventh from Adam, the first of all the prophets prophesied saying "Behold, the Lord cometh with ten thousands of His saints to execute judgment upon all" (Jude 14-15). From his day to the first coming of the Lord all the prophets bore witness to the certainty of this same appearance in glory, and He Himself took it up, for all His words as to His coming in the Synoptic Gospels have His coming in glory in view. In John's Gospel only is the coming FOR His saints alluded to and that was to comfort their hearts. When they sorrowed at the thought of His departure, He said, "I will come again and receive you unto Myself, that where I am, there ye may be also" (chapter 14:3). The Acts of the Apostles presents the Appearing and not the Rapture. It is the burden of the angelic message in chapter 1, which was the first message sent to earth from the Glory after the Lord had entered there. "This same Jesus, which is taken up from you into Heaven, shall so come in like manner as ye have seen Him go into Heaven" (verse 11). Peter takes up the same witness in speaking to the Jews in chapter 3, and very specially in speaking to Gentiles in chapter 10. "He commanded us to preach unto the people, and to testify that it is He which was ordained of God to be the Judge of the quick and dead" (verse 42). And Paul also addressing Gentiles in chapter 17, says, "God now commandeth all men everywhere to repent: because He hath appointed a day in which He will judge the world in righteousness by that Man whom He hath ordained: whereof He hath given assurance to all men, in that He raised Him from the dead" (verses 30-31). It is extremely interesting and instructive that in these two great sermons to Gentiles recorded for us in the Acts, the coming of the Lord as the Judge is so prominent. Gospel preachers should make a note of that.

Question: *Do you think that the angel's message in Acts chapter 1 has in view the appearing of the Lord in glory?*

I do not think there can be any doubt about that. It will be the fulfilment of Zechariah 14:4: "His feet shall stand in that day upon the mount of Olives", for it was from thence that He went up; and if we link up these two Scriptures with Matthew 24:16: "Then let him that is in Judea flee into the mountains", we shall see the reason for that instruction, and be impressed with the way that Scripture interprets itself. To this I must refer again.

The Truth of the Rapture

Question: *What place then has the Rapture?*

When the Lord appears in His glory, we are to appear with Him (Colossians 3:4), and it is by the Rapture that we shall be with Him first, in order to come with Him when He appears. To instruct the saints at Thessalonica as to this was the object of the Apostle in writing his first Epistle to them. They had turned to God from idols, to serve the living and true God, and to WAIT FOR HIS SON FROM HEAVEN (1 Thessalonians 1:9-10), *i.e.*, they were looking for the Appearing of the Lord in glory, and knew nothing as yet of the Rapture. Meanwhile their friends were dying, some of them suffering martyrdom for their faith, and they were sorrowing for them, for they evidently thought that being dead they would miss the glory of the coming of the Lord. To comfort them in this sorrow and to remove it, the Apostle wrote, "I would not have you ignorant, brethren, concerning them that are asleep, that ye sorrow not as others that have no hope. For if we believe that Jesus died and rose again, even so them also which sleep in Jesus will God bring with Him", *i.e.*, when God brings in Jesus in all His glory as the King of kings, and the Judge of quick and dead, those who have fallen asleep through Jesus are to come also, and appear with Him. God will bring them with Him; His word is pledged here as to that. But how will it come about? How glorious is the answer to that question! "For this we say unto you by THE WORD OF THE LORD, that we which are alive and remain unto the coming of the Lord shall not prevent (shall not have any precedence of) them which are asleep. For the Lord Himself shall descend from heaven with a shout, with the voice of the archangel, and the trump of God: and the dead in Christ shall rise first: then we which are alive and remain shall be caught up together with them in the clouds to meet the Lord in the air: and so shall we ever be with the Lord" (1 Thessalonians 4:13-17).

Question: *That is a very wonderful word if we are to take it literally. Must we do that?*

How else can we take it? It is the Word of the Lord. It is such an astounding thing that in making it known the Lord has met the incredulity that would naturally arise in our minds as to it, by giving a special revelation from Himself as to it; so that, in the passage we have more than inspiration by the Holy Ghost, we have that certainly, but what Paul was here inspired by the Holy Ghost to write, he had first of all received from the Lord, and it is the Lord's own word that has been passed on to us, to be received by us in simple faith.

THE LAW OF GRAVITATION

Question: *But it is said that such a thing is both unreasonable and impossible, and some who would not deny the resurrection from the dead, cannot accept the catching up of the living. It is said that the law of gravitation would prevent such an event. How would you meet that?*

I should say first of all that even though we could not explain this word at all, yet since the Lord has spoken it we should believe it, for what is impossible with man is possible with God, and the Word of the Lord is greater than the law of gravitation. But the law of gravitation presents no difficulty to faith or to the one who humbly reads and studies the Word of God. It is a *natural* law, and operates according to the design and decree of the great Creator, but it operates in the physical world and controls natural bodies. It is a natural law for natural bodies, but the Word of God tells us that our natural bodies are to be changed into spiritual bodies. Let us look at the passages that speak of this. Philippians 3:20-21: "For our conversation (citizenship) is in heaven; from whence also we look for the Saviour, the Lord Jesus Christ: who shall change our vile body (body of humiliation), that it may be fashioned like unto His glorious body, according to the working whereby He is able to subdue all things unto Himself." And again in 1 Corinthians 15:51-53: "Behold I shew you a mystery; we shall not all sleep, but we shall all be changed, in a moment, in the twinkling of an eye, at the last trump: for the trumpet shall sound, and the dead shall be raised incorruptible, and we shall be changed. For this corruptible must put on incorruption, and this mortal must put on immortality." These Scriptures have to do with this great event, the changing and catching up of the saints of God to Heaven, and at this point in our study the change is the important consideration. Natural laws control natural bodies, but our bodies are to be changed into bodies of glory like Christ's own body: the natural is to give place to the spiritual, and mortality is to be swallowed up of life (2 Corinthians 5:4), and what sort of laws will control glorified and spiritual bodies, think you? Not natural laws surely, but spiritual laws, the laws of the glory of God, and the greatest of all spiritual laws is that Christ is the centre of God's universe, and He will draw us to Himself and hold us there for ever. So that the law of gravitation need not stumble our faith in the Word of the Lord. It will continue to operate, when we have clean gone from under its power.

Question: *Are there any events recorded in the Bible that would help us as to this?*

Yes. "By faith Enoch was translated that he should not see death; and was not found, because God had translated him" (Hebrews 11:5). And Elijah was rapt up into heaven in a whirlwind, accompanied by a chariot and horses of fire (2 Kings 2:11). And our Lord Himself was taken up, and a cloud received Him out of the sight of His disciples (Acts 1:9). The law of gravitation did not hinder these three great witnesses to the power of God, that subdues death and every other force to His own will. And here the fact of His power should be emphasised. This change in our living bodies is to be effected by His power, the power of our risen, glorified Lord, and it is that power whereby He is able to subdue all things unto Himself, as Philippians 3:21 tells us. No force, natural or physical, in the heavens, the earth, or nether regions can withstand that power.

Question: *When the Scripture speaks of the spiritual body in contrast to the natural (1 Corinthians 15:44), does it mean that we shall be simply spirits?*

No, a spiritual body, or a body of glory, is a body, and a body is substance, and spirit is not substance. It means that we shall have bodies suited to the Glory in contrast to our present bodies which are suited to the earth, or natural life. We are to be clothed upon with our house which is from heaven (2 Corinthians 5); the character, power, glory, and beauty of the changed bodies will be heavenly; it will be the beauty of the Lord. The flesh and blood life will give way to the spiritual and heavenly life, and our bodies will be in every way suited to that life, but they will be bodies. The contrast is not between what is material and what is unsubstantial, but between what is natural and what is spiritual.

"WAITING FOR THE COMING"

Will all Who are Christ's be Caught Up at His Coming for His Saints?

What the Scriptures state.

What about "them that look for Him"?

There are no contradictions in the Scriptures.

His coming is for all that are Christ's.

If it is taught that all saints will be caught up, will it not make Christians indifferent as to their conduct?

"WAITING FOR THE COMING"

Will all Who are Christ's be Caught Up at His Coming for His Saints?

Question: *We are to discuss the appearing of the Lord, but so many questions arise in regard to the Rapture side of His coming, that we ought not to leave it until they are answered. Will all the saints be caught up at the Rapture?*

Most certainly. I know that many devoted Christians deny it, but I am persuaded that they do not rightly divide the Word of Truth, and they have not perceived the greatness and the glory and the indivisible unity of the Church—Christ's own Assembly. They do not distinguish between the Rapture and the Appearing. Let us see what are the actual words of Scripture. 1 Corinthians 15 does not speak of the Rapture of the saints to Heaven, but of the resurrection of the dead in Christ, and of the changing of the living, which precede the Rapture, verse 23 says: "Every man in his own order, Christ the firstfruits; afterward they that are Christ's at His coming"—not a few of these only, or a selected company from among them, but "they that are Christ's". Again addressing the living saints, who shall be alive and remaining here at the coming of the Lord, he says, "We shall not all sleep, but *we shall ALL be changed*" (verse 51). 1 Thessalonians 4:15-16 divides the saints into two classes only, those that are "the dead in Christ", and "we which are alive and remain". There are no saints outside those two classes, and they are to be "CAUGHT UP TOGETHER". None are to be left behind. One glorious eternally united company will be caught up to be for ever with the Lord, not because they have been faithful, but because, on the sure basis of His all-atoning blood, they have been made meet for that destiny by the sovereign grace of the Father (Colossians 1:12-14).

The saints of this great period of grace are indwelt by the Spirit of God, and baptised into *one body*. They are the church, or assembly—which word more truly expresses the truth—and when viewed from this side the thought that only a certain selected, faithful few will be caught up, becomes most repugnant. "Christ loved the church, and gave Himself for it"—not that it might be a mutilated church, part of it in Heaven, and part of it on earth passing through the tribulation in that day of His glory—but that "He might present it to Himself a glorious church, not having spot or wrinkle, or any such thing" (Ephesians 5:25-27). Between the Rapture and the Appearing the marriage of the Lamb will take place in the Glory, and the Lamb's wife, which the church is to be, must be in the Glory before the marriage can take place (Revelation 19).

"Unto Them that Look for Him"

Question: *But what about such a passage as Hebrews 9:28, "Unto them that look for Him shall He appear the second time without sin unto salvation"? Does not that seem to teach that He will only appear to the faithful watchers?*

It most certainly does so teach, but it has in view just as certainly the Appearing and not the Rapture, as it clearly states. While the Hebrew epistle sets forth Christian doctrine, room is left here and there for the blessing of Israel as a people on earth. Several instances of this could be cited, but chapter 8 is a very clear and definite one. The Covenant there is certainly not made with Christians; it is the new covenant that is still to be made with the house of Israel. And I believe that the statement in chapter 9:28 has Israel in view also. The Lord appeared once in their midst, not to deliver them from their enemies, but to be offered to bear the sins of many. The expression, *"The sins of many"* reminds us of the Matthew aspect of the Lord's Supper, which is distinctly Jewish in its bearing and different from the way it is presented by Luke; it carries us back to Isaiah 53, where the Lord is said to "bare the sins of many", and to "justify many", the "many" referring definitely to the saved remnant of Israel. He is to *appear* the second time, apart altogether from the question of sin, for their salvation.

The thought is that of the appearing of the High Priest, after he had taken the blood of the sin offering into the Holiest. The people stood without earnestly looking for him to appear, for they could have no assurance that propitiation for their sins had been made and accepted until he did appear to bless them.

When the remnant of Israel is awakened to their sin and need, after the Rapture of the church to Heaven, they will look for the appearing of their Messiah-priest, and they will not know that He has made propitiation for their sins until He does appear. He has passed into the heavens—into the Holiest, and the Christian does not wait outside that place of high privilege until He appears, but he has the title to go in now, as Hebrews 10:19-22 tells us. Israel will never have this great privilege. But full of sorrow for their sins (see Zechariah 12:10-14), they will wait amidst the miseries of the Tribulation for the appearing of their great Saviour, and their repentance and faith will not be in vain, for as they look for Him He will appear unto their salvation. He will not appear to take up the question of their sins, but to show them by His wounds that "He was wounded for their transgressions" at His first coming, and that He has made a full propitiation for them; and to deliver them from their oppressors. Consider that interpretation of this passage and I believe it will commend itself to you.

Question: *But it is argued that if all Christians are to be caught up at the coming of the Lord, irrespective of their faithfulness, they may be quite easy and indifferent as to their lives and service. What about that side of the question?*

It runs on the same line as the slander which was flung at Paul when he taught the sovereign, unmerited grace of God. He was charged with teaching, "Let us do evil that good may come" (Romans 3:8), and again when he showed that where sin abounded grace did much more abound, the question arose: "Shall we continue in sin that grace may abound?" (Romans 6:1). But grace works in the exact opposite way to that, and the Rapture will be the outcome of sovereign grace and divine love. Our responsibility is not overlooked, but that is taken up in relation to the Appearing, as we have yet to see, but the thought of the Lord's scrutiny of our lives, solemn and sobering as it is, is not the greatest incentive to holy living, and to devotion to Himself. "The love of Christ constraineth us" (2 Corinthians 5:14), Paul said, and it is His love to His own church that will be wonderfully expressed when He catches it up to Himself in the Glory.

The truth of the Rapture is more for the heart than the head. It is as a wonderful secret that we who love the Lord are to cherish, a secret that will keep us from conformity with the world and compromise with sin if we truly keep it. Take the words that are used to convey it to us: "I will come again and receive *you unto Myself*, that where I am, there YE may be also" (John 14:3). "So shall we ever be with the Lord" (1 Thessalonians 4:17). Truly he that hath this hope in Him will purify himself even as He is pure. At the Rapture the Lord will come as the Bridegroom, and what could appeal to the heart of the Bride more strongly than that? It is as the Bridegroom that He says, "Surely, I come quickly. Amen." His last word to His church in Holy Scripture. There can be only one response to that, and it is, "Even so, Come, Lord Jesus."

"WAITING FOR THE COMING"

"Surely, I Come Quickly"

What did the Lord mean by "coming quickly"?

The shout of the Lord, and the Archangel's voice, and the trump of God.

Why the Lord will meet His church in the air.

The last Trump.

"WAITING FOR THE COMING"

"Surely, I Come Quickly"

Question: *Regarding the Coming of the Lord Jesus for His church which we have been considering: four times in the Revelation we read, "I come quickly." Some of us can't understand this, for nearly 2,000 years is not quickly. How do you explain that?*

First, let us be impressed with the fact that it is the Lord Himself who is speaking, it is not even an apostle delivering a message from Him; the words are His own. "I will come again", He says in John 14. "I come quickly", He says in the Revelation; they are His last words to us. If we grasp the fact that they are His own words to those He loves we shall begin to understand them with the heart. Let me illustrate: A mother must leave her children for a while; as she bids them farewell she says, "I'll be back soon", and if she has the opportunity of sending them a message the burden of it is, "I'll see you soon." If she writes a letter to them, instructing them as to what to do during her absence, she closes it with the words, "I'm coming quickly." Why? Because she knows that there is a great yearning in those young hearts; they won't be fully happy and satisfied until they see their mother again, and she knows that no word that she could send them will be more prized by them. But there is another and a deeper reason. Her children are in her heart; she yearns for them; nothing will satisfy her but having them with her again, and nothing will hinder her when her business is done from hastening to them; she will not tarry then. It is thus, we believe, with the Lord. The "quickly" is in His heart; He will not tarry a moment longer than is necessary. "For yet a little while, and He that shall come will come, and will *not* tarry" (Hebrews 10:37). Do we understand that? Unless we have left our first love we shall understand it and we shall cherish these last words of His to us, and continually in our hearts there will be this response, "Even so, Come, Lord Jesus."

THE SHOUT OF THE LORD, THE ARCHANGEL'S VOICE AND THE TRUMP OF GOD

Question: *1 Thessalonians 4:16 speaks of the shout of the Lord, the voice of the archangel, and the trump of God. What are we to understand by these three things?*

We shall have no difficulty as to the shout of the Lord. It is the Lord's own shout. As a captain commands his army, so the Lord will command and assemble the countless number of His saints, dead and living, to meet Him in the air, and there will be "our gathering together unto Him" (2 Thessalonians 2:1). There will be authority and triumph in that shout, but more. I listened with great pleasure to a servant of the Lord, insisting that it would be a shout of joy. For nearly 2,000 years the Lord has waited for this moment, for the moment when He shall receive and present to Himself His blood-bought church—this is the hour of His patience—but the waiting time will be over when He rises up in His power; and the shout will be a shout of joy, of long pent-up desire, if we may speak thus in deepest reverence. The shout of the Lord will have

His saints solely in view, and that shout will have an instant answer; in a moment, in the twinkling of an eye we shall be with Him.

The archangel is Michael (Jude 9), and he is Israel's prince (Daniel 10:21): the great spiritual power that stands for Israel. Whenever he is mentioned by name it is in relation to events in the career of that nation (see Jude 9 and Revelation 12). I suggest then that the voice of the archangel will have to do with the gathering of Israel. The trump of God seems to be more universal, it will affect all mankind. If this is the interpretation, we have here three widening circles. (1) The Church, (2) Israel, (3) All men. All will be affected by this great event. The effect will not be simultaneous in these circles, the wheels will move slower in regard to Israel and mankind, but they will begin to move then. There will be as I have said, an instant response from the church; the work will be slower in regard to Israel, but from that moment the nation will begin to move towards the land of Canaan and their preparation for the return of the Messiah will begin; and every nation will be affected also. It will not be until the Son of Man sits on the throne of His glory, that all nations will be gathered before Him, but the trump of God, which sounds forth at the coming of the Lord, will secure that.

What I should like all to see is, that everything awaits the catching up of the church out of this world; until that takes place all the promises of God in regard to Israel and the nations of men are held up, they cannot be fulfilled, but when that does take place, events will move swiftly to the great and glorious appearing of the Lord, and the voice of the archangel and the trump of God will have accomplished their great work. We need a fuller conception of the importance of the church in God's ways. It is the brightest and most cherished prize that Christ will secure from among men, and until He has secured it—complete, perfect, glorious, without spot or blemish—none of God's plans proceed to their appointed end; but when it has been secured, to share with the coming King all His glory, then God will make no more delay, and Israel and the nations will bow the knee to Christ; God's kingdom will come.

Why the Lord will meet His Church in the Air

Question: *Why are the saints not caught right up into the Father's house? Why should the Lord come to meet them in the air?*

They *will* be caught right up into the Father's house, of course. John 14 assures us of that, but the Lord will come forth to meet them to conduct them into that place that He has prepared for them. His coming forth to meet them shows the love He has for them, and the honour that He puts upon them. As a king goes forth to meet his royal bride when the news reaches him that she has left her own land for his, so will the Lord come forth to meet His bride.

But that He should meet her in the air is full of significance. The air is the seat of Satan's power; he is the prince of the power of the air (Ephesians 2:2). It is from the air—the heavenlies—that the principalities and powers and rulers of the darkness of this world and the spiritual wickedness operate (Ephesians 6:12), and it is there that the Lord will meet His own. Suppose a great king at war with another were to send a message to his army in a distant field of operations, saying that he would meet them in the capital of the enemy's country. Well, we should say, he will need to crush the enemy's power before he can do that, and if he does it, it will be the most conclusive evidence of his complete victory. It is just so in this matter. The enemy is a defeated foe; the power of the devil has been annulled. Would he not, were he able, prevent the Lord from receiving His own into glory? He certainly would; but it is in the very capital of his dark dominion, in the region from which he now operates against the church, and holds men in darkness, that the Lord will meet His saints, and they, sharing His triumph and joy, will pass through the air and into the Father's house to be for ever with the Lord.

Consequent upon this manifest triumph of the Lord over him, the devil is to be cast out of his present seat of power in the heavenlies. Revelation 12 tells us of this, and that he will come down to earth "having great wrath". We can understand that; since Pentecost his power and subtlety have been concentrated on the church. The Apostle Paul wrote to the Corinthians, "I have espoused you to one husband, that I may present you as a chaste virgin to Christ", and this is true of the whole church, but, he added, "I fear, lest by any means, as the serpent beguiled Eve through his subtilty, so your minds should be corrupted from the simplicity that is in Christ" (2 Corinthians 11:2-3). This has been Satan's endeavour; with this end in view he has changed himself into an angel of light, and when this has failed, he has gone about as a roaring lion seeking whom he may devour. His counsels and determination and efforts have been to rob Christ of His church, but the gates of hell shall not prevail against it, said the Lord, and here we see that word fulfilled, and in spite of the utmost that Satan can do, the church passes clean through His domain, holy and without blame, having neither spot nor wrinkle nor any such thing, to be for ever for Christ, as a bride adorned for her husband. When the devil sees that and realises the fulness of Christ's victory, he may well have great wrath.

THE LAST TRUMP

Question: *In 1 Corinthians 15:52 we read of "the last trump". Is this the same as "the trump of God"? If not, what are we to understand by it?*

I do not think these two are the same. The last trump has been explained to be a military allusion. In the Roman armies three trumpet blasts were given when they had to move. The first blast meant "pack your baggage"; the second, "fall in"; and the third, "March." If this is the true explanation of the expression, and I believe it is, how significant it is. The Christian is to be standing ready for the final trumpet call. Already he has heard the call of the Gospel, and if he has given a true answer to it he has separated himself from the world, has packed his baggage, and is looking for the Saviour. He is waiting, eagerly, expectantly for the last trump, when in a moment in the twinkling of an eye, the whole triumphant and blood-washed company shall be changed into the glorious likeness to their Lord, and death shall be swallowed up in victory.

Signs of His Coming

The folly of fixing dates.

Will the world be converted by the Gospel?

The calling out of the Church.

Signs of His Coming.

Texts that show the difference between the Rapture and the Appearing.

"WAITING FOR THE COMING"

Signs of His Coming

Question: *What do you say as to fixing dates as to the coming of the Lord?*

The fixing of dates as to the coming of the Lord is a pernicious thing, and those who do it are presumptuous people. The Lord Himself said, "But of that day and that hour knoweth no man, no, nor the angels which are in Heaven, neither the Son, but the Father" (Mark 13:32). Yes, says some one, but we know the year. Indeed? Then why did the Lord add, "Watch and pray: *for ye know not when the time is*" (verse 33), and again, "for *ye know not when the Master of the house cometh*, at even, or at midnight, or at cock-crowing, or in the morning" (verse 35)? To the apostles who have given us the Word of God by the Holy Spirit's inspiration, the Lord said, "It is not for you to know the times and the seasons, which the Father hath put in His own power" (Acts 1:7). If this knowledge was withheld from them in the Father's wisdom, where is there any indication in the Word that it would be revealed to us? These sayings of the Lord have to do with His coming in glory, and they surely abide true in regard to it. The church period has intervened, it will close with the Rapture, but not a word or a hint is given in relation to the Rapture that the time of it may be known. Days, months, years and numbers are given in the Scriptures, but they have their relation to Israel and the earth, and are all in abeyance until the heavenly company is secured and caught up, then the clock of prophecy will start again, and God's calendar will justify itself. Meanwhile we must accept the words of the Lord, and wait and watch and work.

WILL THE WORLD BE CONVERTED BY THE GOSPEL?

Question: *It is a popular notion that the world is to be converted by the preaching of the Gospel or by the spread of righteousness, and that then, and not till then, the Lord will come. How does that fit in with the Scriptures?*

It does not fit in with the Scriptures at all; it has no foundation or support in them. To quote a few texts will be enough to show how false it is. "Behold, He cometh with clouds; and every eye shall see Him, and they also that pierced Him: and *all kindreds of the earth shall wail because of Him*" (Revelation 1:7). If it is to a converted world that He comes, why should all kindreds of the earth wail because of Him? If they were all converted they would most surely rejoice at His coming, and receive Him with acclamation. But it is because He is COMING AS THE JUDGE that they will fear. "Enoch, the seventh from Adam, prophesied of this, saying, Behold, the Lord cometh with ten thousands of His saints to execute judgment upon all, and to convince all that are ungodly among them of all their ungodly deeds ..." (Jude 14-15). He is coming to judge because the world has not been converted by the Gospel, and because the only way in which righteousness can be established on the earth is by judgment. This is made solemnly clear by another Scripture, "The Lord Jesus shall be revealed from Heaven, with His mighty angels, in flaming fire taking vengeance on them that know not God, and that obey not the Gospel of our Lord Jesus Christ: who shall be punished with everlasting destruction from the presence of the Lord and the glory of His power" (2 Thessalonians 1:7-9). There are a host of confirmatory texts, but one other will be enough. "And the kings of the earth, and the great men, and the rich men, and the chief captains, and the mighty men, and every bond man, and every free man, hid themselves in the dens and the rocks of the mountains; and said to the mountains and rocks, Fall on us, and hide us from the face of Him that sitteth on the throne, and from THE WRATH OF THE LAMB: for the great day of His wrath is come; and who shall be able to stand?" (Revelation 6:15-17). Could the Lamb be wroth with a converted world? And would converted men cry out for a hiding place from Him? Yet here men in every station of life are reduced to the common level of abject terror at the very thought of His coming.

Question: *Then what is the Gospel for if not to convert the world?*

It has been sent into the world to gather a people out of the world for the Lord's Name. This comes out clearly in Acts 15:14: "God at the first did visit the Gentiles, to take out of them a people for His Name." Those who believe the Gospel are delivered from this present evil world, according to the will of God and our Father (Galatians 1:4). The distinction between the disciples of the Lord and the world is clearly given in the Lord's own words, "Because I have chosen you out of the world, therefore the world hateth you" (John 15:19), and throughout the chapters 14-17 of John's Gospel. Every true believer on the Lord Jesus is a "called out" one, sanctified in Christ Jesus, and belongs to His church that He is soon to catch away out of the world for ever; they look for mercy and salvation at His coming; while for the world there is judgment—"a certain looking for of judgment and fiery indignation, which shall devour the adversaries" (Hebrews 10:27).

It is of the utmost importance that we should understand that the Gospel has called us out of the world to Heaven; having believed it, our names are written there; our citizenship is there, and it is from thence that "we look for the Saviour, who shall change our bodies of humiliation, and fashion them like unto His own body of glory, according to the working whereby He is able to subdue all things unto Himself" (Philippians 3:20-21). At the first stage of His coming again, when He will catch away from the world His blood-bought saints, He will get something *out of the world;* at His Appearing in glory with His saints He will do something *in the world.*

Question: *Why do you stress the fact of our being called out of the world so much?*

Because the true character of the Church cannot be understood unless this is understood, and unless we understand the character of our calling, we cannot be true to it; and neither shall we understand the prophetic Scriptures, nor rightly divide the Word of truth, if we fail to see the unique character of the Church and its calling. We have been made partakers of "a heavenly calling" (Hebrews 3:1). Our blessings are in "the heavenly places in Christ Jesus" (Ephesians 1:3). Our hope is laid up for us in heaven (Colossians 1:5), and we are to set our affections upon the things that are there (chapter 3:1-4). And finally the Lord said in His prayer to His Father, "They are not of the world even as I am not of the world" (John 17:14). If the Church had held fast to this great fact it would not have settled down in the world, and it would have kept free from those entanglements that have bound it a captive to the world's schemes and ways, and made it grind at its mills, like blinded Samson at the mills of the Philistines. Thousands of earnest Christians are wasting their energies and time in efforts to improve the world that cannot be improved, because they do not see and realise their heavenly calling, when they might be building for eternity—building in relation to the chief corner Stone, which has been rejected by the world (Acts 4:11-12; 1 Peter 2:6-8). That building, which groweth unto an holy temple in the Lord (Ephesians 2:19-22), is most surely nearing its completion; when it is completed it will be caught up to Heaven. The door will be closed, and all those who have had nothing but an empty profession, will be shut out, and will knock without success at the closed door (Luke 13:25-30).

SIGNS OF HIS COMING

Question: *We have heard much talk about signs of the Lord's coming again, especially during the [first world] war and since. Ought we to be looking for such?*

There are certainly sure signs that we are in the last days, but these are not "wars and rumours of wars, earthquakes in divers places and famines and pestilences; and fearful sights and great signs" (Luke 21). All these are to take place before the *Appearing of the Lord in His glory* and have nothing to do with the coming of the Lord for His Church. Some have allowed their imagination to run riot as to such things and as to sensational events in the political world. So, in the rise of Mussolini, and the efforts of the League of Nations, they have seen the Beast of Revelation 13 and the ten kingdoms. It is a superficial knowledge of Scripture that leads them into these errors, and the inability to rightly divide the word of truth. The Beast is to rise up out of the anarchy and confusion that will follow the catching up of the Church to Heaven. 2 Thessalonians 2 clearly shows us that neither he nor Anti-Christ can be manifested until that event has taken place, and the kings will have their power given to them at the same time for one hour—a brief period (Revelation 17:12). The presence of the Holy Spirit in the Church on earth holds back the full development of these evil forces, and He will continue to hold them back until He be taken out of the way. Signs of this sort and such as are given by the Lord in Matthew 24 and Luke 21, will be a help to the godly Jewish remnant awaiting the coming of their Messiah.

But the Scriptures do instruct us as to the character of the last days—"Men shall be lovers of their own selves ... lovers of pleasure more than lovers of God; having a form of godliness, but denying the power thereof" (2 Timothy 3:1-5). "Knowing this first, that there shall come in the last days scoffers, walking after their own lusts, and saying, Where is the promise of His coming?" (2 Peter 3:3-4). And this state of things is in the professing Church. Leaders in the "Christian world" lead great campaigns for Sunday pleasures and scoff at the teaching of the coming again of the Lord; these turn away from truth, having itching ears (2 Timothy 4:3-4); and their presence in the professing Church and their activities are a sure sign that we are in the last times. Sad signs indeed they are. But there is another and a brighter one; it is the awakening of desire in the hearts of multitudes of the saints of God to see the Lord; they are being recovered to the truth of His Coming Again. The Spirit and *the bride* say, Come. Whenever there is recovery to first love to the Lord, there will be this longing for His return, and it is for this recovery, this true revival, that we should be praying and labouring, for this is the surest of all signs that His coming is near. The more definitely we are recovered to this true, normal Christian state, the more we shall talk of the Lord, and it will not be signs that will occupy our thoughts but Himself—the bright and morning Star.

Those who have this hope in Christ will purify themselves, even as He is pure; they will separate themselves from those evil men whose presence in the professing Church are a sign of the last days, and they will draw together as those did at the close of Old Testament history: "Then they that feared the LORD spake often one to another; and the LORD hearkened, and heard, and a book of remembrance was written before Him for them that feared the LORD, and that thought upon His Name. And they shall be Mine, saith the LORD of hosts, in that day when I make up My jewels" (Malachi 3:16-17).

But notice, in this connection, "Then shall ye return, and discern between the righteous and the wicked, between him that serveth God and him that serveth Him not" (verse 18). Nothing will promote holiness of walk and separation from evil men like this great hope of the coming of our Saviour. It will make us like unto men that wait for their lord.

THE DIFFERENCE BETWEEN THE RAPTURE AND THE APPEARING

Question: *Will you cite texts to show that there is this distinction between the Rapture and the Appearing, and that when the Lord does appear His church will not be on the earth? In 1 Timothy 6:13-14 Paul exhorts Timothy to "keep this commandment ... until the Appearing of our Lord Jesus Christ", which seems to support the idea that the church will be here until the Appearing.*

"WAITING FOR THE COMING"

There are many passages of Scripture which show that when the Lord appears in glory His saints will appear with Him. Some of these are: "When Christ, Who is our life, shall appear, then shall ye also appear *with Him* in glory" (Colossians 3:4), "The coming of our Lord Jesus Christ *with* all His saints" (1 Thessalonians 3:13), "Them also which sleep in Jesus will God bring *with Him*" (1 Thessalonians 4:14), "The Lord cometh *with* ten thousands of His saints" (Jude 14), "They that are *with Him* are called, and chosen, and faithful" (Revelation 17:14), "The armies which were in heaven followed Him upon white horses, clothed in fine linen, white and clean" (Revelation 19:14). It is clear from these Scriptures that He does not find His Church on earth at His Appearing, but that it comes with Him; how this is possible is unfolded, as we have seen, in 1 Thessalonians 4:16-17.

The charge to Timothy in the passage quoted, emphasizes the responsibility of the Lord's servants to hold the fort for the Lord until He returns, to establish His kingdom and authority. This is one side of our witness and service; we represent Him while He is absent from the world because we know that He is coming back to it. This is a most important part of our testimony to the world. Our testimony is really threefold: He has been here in grace, He is not here for He was rejected, He is coming back again in power and glory to judge and to rule in righteousness. Meanwhile His servants, of whom Timothy was a pattern, must hold the truth in its spotless purity, without compromise, in subjection to the Lord. When the Church has been taken out of the world, God will bring to light others who will hold the standard aloft and keep the light burning until the Appearing of the Lord.

SIGNS OF HIS COMING

Question: *You think then that the Lord will find faithful servants on the earth when He appears. If these are not of the Church, who will they be?*

He will, but they will be saints of the Jewish people, a remnant in whose hearts the Spirit will work after the Rapture of the Church. He will appear for their salvation. With the Rapture of the Church, the Spirit who dwells in it will also be taken out of the way. Then the man of sin and Antichrist will be revealed (2 Thessalonians 2; Revelation 13), and the great tribulation will begin. All the world will be tried by it, but the Jewish nation, because they rejected their Messiah, will suffer most, and in this nation, a faithful remnant will appear, who shall turn to God and suffer more than all, and that even from their compatriots. The Lord will appear for their salvation, as many scriptures tell. "Hear the Word of the LORD, ye that tremble at His Word; your brethren that hated you, that cast you out for My Name's sake, said, Let the LORD be glorified. But He shall appear to your joy, and they shall be ashamed" (Isaiah 66:5). "Unto them that look for Him shall He appear the second time without sin unto salvation" (Hebrews 9:28). "Then shall appear the sign of the Son of Man in heaven: and then shall all the tribes of the earth mourn, and they shall see the Son of Man coming in the clouds of heaven with power and great glory. And He shall send His angels with a great sound of a trumpet, and *they shall gather together His elect* from the four winds, from one end of heaven to the other" (Matthew 24:30-31).

"WAITING FOR THE COMING"

Waiting, Watching, Working

What bearing has Luke 12 on those who are expecting the coming of the Lord?

Does watching indicate something greater than waiting?

The Rewards.

What about the unfaithful servant?

"WAITING FOR THE COMING"

Waiting, Watching, Working

Question: *What bearing has Luke 12:34-48 upon us, who are looking for the Rapture of the church at the first stage of the Lord's coming?*

It sets before us in the Lord's own words, our responsibility during His absence from this world, and the rewards for faithfulness. Three things are to mark us: readiness, expectancy and activity; we are to be waiting, watching, and working.

Question: *What is the meaning of the figures used: loins girded and lights burning?*

The lights burning show that it is night, the night of the Lord's absence, and the tendency is to ungird and go to sleep at night, but in a spiritual sense we must not do that; for while we are *in* the night we are not *of* it, but "we are children of the day ... therefore let us not sleep, as do others; but let us watch and be sober" (1 Thessalonians 5:5-6). The loins girded and the light burning indicate readiness to move at the word of the Lord; there must be no scrambling and scurrying when He comes; we are to be like unto men that wait for their Lord.

"WAITING FOR THE COMING"

Question: *Does the watching of verse 37, to which a special blessedness is attached, indicate something better than simply waiting?*

Both have their place, but watching means expectancy, the heart is engaged. A servant might be quite ready for his master's return, as simply obeying a command, but if he is watching, it shows that his master's return is absorbing his thoughts. But with the Christian the two must go together; if the heart is not right towards the Lord, the loins will become ungirded and the light will grow dim.

Question: *What of the next section, where the faithful servant feeds the household, and is also called "blessed": is that evidence of greater devotion?*

It shows us the servant in his activities and runs on with the waiting and watching; the three things give a complete description of a servant altogether pleasing to the Lord. I might illustrate these three things. The mother of a family has been compelled to leave her home for a while, and it and the younger children are left in charge of Mary, her mother's trusted daughter. She has told them that she will not tarry when her business is finished, and they are expecting her daily. With this expectation bright in her heart Mary keeps the home clean and tidy, so that when the mother does return she may find *everything ready*, the home clean, the children dressed and waiting. But they are not only ready but expectant; often they run to the door or peer out of the window for the first sight of the returning mother, and as the days go by Mary becomes more eager than them all. Yet she does not forget her mother's wishes; she sees that the children are fed and she does not allow them to forget that mother is coming; she actively cares for her mother's interests, idling not for a moment. Between her journeys to the door and window, she slips first into this room and then into that, to see that nothing is out of place, and she keeps her eye on her brothers and sisters, for she does not want to be ashamed of them before her mother when she returns; she waits and watches like them all, but she diligently works as well. She does everything as she feels her mother would if she were there. She is faithful to her trust. Blessed is Mary when her mother returns. She has a twofold joy; her mother is back again, and smiles her approval on her little daughter.

The Rewards

Question: *Do the rewards of which the Lord speaks show the measure of His appreciation of the faithfulness of His servants?*

Yes. I will continue my parable to illustrate this. Mary has the joy of her mother's presence and the satisfaction of her mother's approbation. But now the mother's turn has come. She makes Mary sit down at the table, and all the children, for they were all alike longing and watching for her return, and she brings out the good things she has brought for them; they feast together, but the mother serves. Her delight in being with her children, and the pleasure in their love that made them long and watch for her return, makes her their servant now. But what a reward that feast is to Mary; she has it as a secret understanding between her mother and herself, and a special mark of her mother's approval. This is the way the Lord proposes to recompense His watching servants in verse 37. "Verily I say unto you, that He shall gird Himself, and make them to sit down to meat, and will come forth and serve them."

Question: *What is the difference between that, and "He will make him ruler over all that he hath" (verse 44)?*

The service of love rendered to His watching servants, seems to be *inside the house*. It is a private festival that the world won't see. It is love answering to love. It is love in the hearts of His servants that leads to this expectancy and watching, and love in the heart of the faithful Lord will lead Him to show His appreciation of that love that did not forget Him during His absence. But the making him ruler of all that he hath is *a public honour* for public service; the servant is rewarded openly for his faithful service by a place of trust in the kingdom. Both are blessed, but the latter would not be greatly valued without the former.

Question: *Before leaving this Scripture, please explain what the Lord says about the unfaithful servants in verses 45-48.*

The servant evinces his reality by his conduct and vice versa. Many are servants by profession who are not so in reality and in heart, but a man's conduct shows what is in his heart. This servant says *in his heart*, "My Lord delayeth his coming." He does not openly deny that He will come, but he defers the coming and casts off the true servant character, and lords it over God's heritage, as though the day of reckoning would never come. To such a servant the Lord's coming will be sudden, unexpected; He will come as a thief in the night to him, as He will to the world. He is an evil servant (Matthew 24:48), and shall have his portion with the unbelievers, because he is an unbeliever. The solemn words stand as a warning to each and all, yet how clearly there is foretold in them the unfaithfulness of the professing church; how soon in its history it lost the hope and desire for the Lord's return; and left its first love, and settled down in the world to eat and drink with the drunken, as though it belonged to the world and the night (1 Thessalonians 5:7), and then to lord it over kings and princes, and to persecute the faithful servants of the Lord. It is the spirit of the world in the professing church and must be a grief to the Lord and all who are faithful to Him, and it will meet with His unsparing judgment at His appearing.

The words as to the faithful and wise steward are an encouragement, for they show that until the Lord does come there will be such, who shall care for His interests and feed His household with wisdom and love. He cares for His household, and has provided abundant food for their spiritual health and strength, and this food has been committed to His stewards. There could be no greater sin on the part of any of His servants than the withholding of this food from those who need it, and no greater service to the Lord than the diligent dispensing of it. Blessed are those servants, whom their Lord when He cometh shall find so doing. Awake ye stewards of the Lord; the time is short; the coming of the Lord draweth nigh.

"WAITING FOR THE COMING"

The Judgment Seat of Christ

When will the faithful servants of the Lord be rewarded?

John 5:24 says that those who believe "shall not come into judgment". What of that?

What will the judgment seat mean for us?

What it means to suffer loss.

Wasted lives; works burnt up.

The unprofitable servant and his doom.

"WAITING FOR THE COMING"

The Judgment Seat of Christ

Question: *You think that the Scriptures teach that the manifestation of the servants of the Lord as to their faithfulness will take place at the Appearing of Christ and not at the Rapture?*

The rewards for faithful service will be *enjoyed* then; and each one will have his place in kingdom glory according to his faithfulness, but the actual manifestation will be at the judgment seat of Christ. Then and there the Lord will scrutinize the works that we have done. The text that speaks definitely of this is 2 Corinthians 5:10, and I give it as it appears in the New Translation (N.Tr.): "For we must all be manifested before the judgment seat of Christ, that each one may receive the things done in the body, according to those he has done, whether it be good or evil." And a passage that naturally links up with this is 1 Corinthians 3:12-15: "Now if any man build upon this foundation gold, silver, precious stones, wood, hay, stubble; every man's work shall be made manifest: for the day shall declare it, because it shall be revealed by fire, and the fire shall try every man's work of what sort it is. If any man's work abide, which he hath built thereupon, he shall receive a reward. If any man's work shall be burned up, he shall suffer loss: but he himself shall be saved; yet so as by fire."

Question: *How do you reconcile these statements with the Lord's own words in John 5:24, that those that believe "shall not come into judgment", as I think the word should be?*

There is really no difficulty in John 5. It is the person that is in question; at the judgment seat of Christ it is the deeds or works. The person of the believer can never come into judgment, for his Saviour who will sit on the judgment seat, suffered in his stead upon the Cross; the judgment is past and the condemnation endured, and the penalty paid, and the believer having passed out of death into life has passed beyond the reach of judgment, being in Christ where there is no condemnation for him (Romans 8:1). Yet his works will be scrutinized, and he will learn what the Lord thinks about his life and ways. Many questions and problems that have arisen in this life, for which we have found no answer, will be answered then, and the full value of all our deeds, according to the Lord's own estimate, will then be shown to us, and we shall be rewarded or suffer loss accordingly. But we shall be then, as I think 2 Corinthians 5 indicates, in our glorified bodies. Nothing can rob us of this and our place in the glory, which is all according to sovereign grace.

WHAT IT MEANS TO SUFFER LOSS

Question: *If we are sure of being in Heaven through the atoning Blood of Christ, how can we be said to suffer loss?*

Suppose two workmen employed by the same master. They both receive full instructions from the master on Monday morning as to their work for the week, instructions so clear that nobody could possibly mistake them. One works consistently and conscientiously to the master's plan, and finishes the work to the master's satisfaction. The other spends one half of the week in pleasing himself, and when he does settle down to work, he pays very scant heed to his master's wishes and does the work as he thinks it ought to be done. It is not difficult to see how different the lot of these two men will be at the end of the week, one will receive a full reward for his labour, the other will suffer loss, for half his week was wasted, and the work of the other half badly done. He would have very little to show for it, and would gain his master's disapproval. So with the Christian, according to his faithfulness or otherwise he will be rewarded, he will receive the things done in the body whether they be good or bad.

Question: *Do you think that there will be Christians in Heaven who will have no works to show at all, whose works will all be burnt up, though they themselves will be saved; yet so as by fire?*

It does not seem possible that any true Christian's life will be entirely barren of fruit, or that all his works will be destroyed. I remember being at a Bible Study, and our subject was 1 Corinthians 3. One brother remarked, "You see it is possible that when we stand before the judgment seat of Christ, all our works may be burnt up, and we ourselves saved, but with nothing to show as a result of our salvation." A brother who had been saved from a life of infamy, and who was a bright example of the saving grace of God, quietly remarked, "And what sort of a salvation would you call that?" He was right if there is no fruit in the life, no good works by which God is glorified, we may well conclude that the grace is not there, for "by their fruits shall ye know them."

Question: *Yet some lives seem sadly wasted, what about them?*

Yes. I knew a young man who as a lad had professed the name of the Lord Jesus, but as he grew up he threw his whole energies into pleasure and sport, and at 29 lay dying. He seemed impervious to anything that was said to him, but one night he had a dream. He was in a room in which were exhibited some beautiful specimens of the wood carver's art, many of his own being among them. Suddenly, as he examined these works of art, the building burst into flames, and he with great difficulty, just managed to escape from the building, as it collapsed in ruins. He was saved by the skin of his teeth. He knew the Scriptures, and two of them flashed into his agitated mind when he awoke. "If any man's work shall be burned, he shall suffer loss; but he himself shall be saved; yet so as by fire" (1 Corinthians 3:15), and "the earth also and the works that are therein shall be burned up" (2 Peter 3:10). It was God's voice to his soul; he saw that he had lived for himself and the world, and his life was a lost life, but, thank God, he made good use of the little while that was left him, and in witnessing to the saving power, and pardoning grace of the Lord he built gold, silver, and precious stones.

Question: *What Scriptures would you quote to prove that the Christian's faithfulness here will be rewarded by a place in the kingdom of the Lord at His Appearing?*

The parables of Matthew 25:14-30, and Luke 19:11-27, and the Lord's words in Luke 12:35-48, and such passages as 2 Timothy 2:12, "If we suffer we shall also reign with Him", and Romans 8:17, "If so be that we suffer with Him, that we may be also glorified together."

The Unfaithful Servant

Question: *Before leaving this subject how would you prove that the unfaithful servant in the parables of Matthew 25 and Luke 19 is an unbeliever and not a true Christian who is shut out of the kingdom for his unfaithfulness?*

Is it conceivable that the Lord would condemn anyone whom He had redeemed by His blood to outer darkness, where there is weeping and gnashing of teeth? But out of the man's own mouth shall he be judged. "I feared thee," he said, "because thou art an austere man." Most surely he did not know his Lord at all; would anyone who knows Him speak thus of Him? Those who know Him, while they deplore their unfaithfulness, bear witness to His patience and tenderness of heart, and readiness to forgive, and it is this knowledge of Him that constrains them to faithful service. The man was a servant in name and by profession only; he had no vital knowledge of the Lord. Alas, there are many such.

"WAITING FOR THE COMING"

The Judgment of the Living and the Dead

A comparison between Matthew 25:31-46 and Revelation 20:11-15.

The Judge of the quick and dead.

The Son of Man on the Throne of His Glory.

The sheep and the goats.

The Great White Throne.

"WAITING FOR THE COMING"

The Judgment of the Living and the Dead

Question: *Please explain Matthew 25:31-46. It is a puzzling passage, and has been interpreted as teaching that there will be one general judgment at which the great division between men will be made, and some have even said that no one can know before then where they will stand, whether on the right hand as sheep, or on the left hand as goats. It seems to be confounded with the judgment of the great white Throne of Revelation 20:11-15.*

A comparison of the two Scriptures in question will show the difference between them.

(1) We must notice that in the great drama of Matthew 25, there will be three companies, and not two, the sheep, the goats, and those whom the Son of Man calls "My brethren"; in the judgment of Revelation 20, there is but one.

(2) It is nations that will be judged, as such, and that certainly means that they will be *living* at the time, for nationalities and all class distinctions cease at death, while in Revelation 20, we learn that it is the *dead* that will stand before the great white Throne.

(3) Matthew 25 contemplates entrance into or exclusion from a kingdom prepared from the foundation of the earth, an earthly kingdom; while the great white Throne will appear when the earth has fled away from the face of Him that sits upon it.

(4) The Judgment of Matthew 25 will be at the beginning of the Lord's earthly kingdom; that of Revelation 20, after those thousand years of peace and prosperity have closed (verse 7).

(5) And finally, it is as Son of Man come in His glory that the Lord will judge according to Matthew 25; but it is as God that He will sit upon the great white Throne to dispose of the wicked dead.

The first time that ever a company of Gentiles heard the Gospel was when Simon Peter preached it in the house of Cornelius of Caesarea, and he told them that the Lord had commanded His servants to preach and to testify that "it was He which was ordained of God to be the Judge of quick and dead" (Acts 10:42). He will judge both, but at different times. Matthew 25 undoubtedly gives us the judgment of at least a considerable number of the quick. As King of kings and Lord of lords, who is called the Faithful and True, and whose Name is the Word of God, He will destroy the whole military power of men (Revelation 19:11-16). All that are found in arms against Him will be instantly smitten at that time and without any trial. Then will follow this judgment of the living nations, and He will carry it out according to His rights as the Son of Man. As Son of David He has supreme rights over Israel. But as Son of Man He will exercise universal dominion, and the first act of His rule will be this great Assize. He will sit on the throne of His glory and

THE JUDGMENT OF THE LIVING AND THE DEAD

award blessing or condemnation according to the desserts of those who stand before Him.

The test and ground of the judgment will be the way "His brethren" have been treated by these nations. I do not think that it can be questioned that these brethren are the Jewish missionaries that will proclaim His coming as King. They will go forth and preach "this Gospel of the kingdom in all the world for a witness to all nations" (Matthew 24:14). Their labours will be a fulfilment of the word in Psalm 68:11: "The Lord gave the word: great was the company of those that published it." These servants of the Lord, whom He will raise up and empower from among the Jews, after the Rapture of the church to heaven, will be "hated of all nations for My Name's sake", as the Lord has foretold (Matthew 24:9); for under the influence of the Beast and the False Prophet men will be set against every thing of God. But the hearts of some will be opened by the grace of God to receive their message and to pity and succour them. These will be those whom the Lord addresses as blessed of His Father, and they will be introduced by Him into the kingdom prepared for them from the foundation of the world. For inasmuch as they did it unto one of the least of His brethren they did it to Him. We may be sure that these nations will be the subjects of God's work of grace, and will be born again, otherwise they could not be the sheep of Christ, nor would they have cared for His servants. The remainder, who will manifest their nature, as enemies of Christ and God, by their indifference to these persecuted missionaries, will be judged as such, and shall go away into everlasting punishment.

The great white Throne judgment will be the last judgment of all, when the dead who have died without mercy from the days of Cain to the last of his kind, shall appear before God. The judgment will be according to eternal, inexorable justice, for the books will be opened. The book of God's most accurate record, and the book of every man's conscience and memory, corroborating all that God has written. Another book also, the book of life, will be opened, and it will be the final test of all. And while every man will be judged there according to their works, that which will irrevocably seal their doom will be that they have no part in the book of life; they are indeed the dead, and this is the second death; for whosoever was not found written in the book of life was cast into the lake of fire.

We may well send up a hymn of heartfelt praise to God that we whose names are written in that book of life can never come into that judgment. And rejoice in these good words of the Lord: "He that heareth My Word and believeth on Him that sent Me, hath everlasting life, and shall not come into condemnation (judgment), but is passed from death unto life" (John 5:24)

The Herald of His Coming

"That the Word of the Lord may run."

The judgment and the blessing at His Appearing: the showers on the new-mown grass.

No judgment as long as the church is on earth.

"The man of sin" and "that wicked one".

The Lord Jesus revealed in flaming fire.

"WAITING FOR THE COMING"

The Herald of His Coming

There is an illuminating word in 2 Thessalonians 3:1. The great Apostle Paul begs the young Christians at Thessalonica to pray that the Word of the Lord may have free course—*or that it may run* (N.Tr.). If we remember that the subject of the two Epistles to the Thessalonians is the coming again of the Lord Jesus, we shall realise how striking and appropriate is this figure of speech. The King is coming, and His herald runs before Him announcing the fact. The Word of the Lord is the herald. It is the Gospel, of course, but not the Gospel as it is so poorly understood and preached by many preachers in these slack days. The Gospel of God (Romans 1) *is concerning His Son, Jesus Christ our Lord*, who is raised up from the dead and set in the place of supremacy at God's right hand, to administer the grace of God from that place of power to all who will receive the Word, until the hour arrives when He shall appear in glory and God shall set Him on His throne in Zion. This was the word that the apostles preached, with the result that those who believed it "turned to God from idols, to serve the living and true God, and *to wait for His Son from Heaven*, whom He raised from the dead, even Jesus, our Deliverer from the wrath to come" (1 Thessalonians 1:9-10).

This Word of the Lord, the herald going before the Lord to announce His coming, is indeed a word of grace, the Gospel of our salvation, giving all who believe it a heavenly hope, but it is also an imperative word, it claims and commands obedience. It is like the herald that went before Joseph in Egypt, crying, "Bow the knee" (Genesis 41:43), and those that refuse to obey it, "that obey not the Gospel of our Lord Jesus Christ" are to be "punished with everlasting destruction from the presence of the Lord, and from the glory of His power" at His appearing (2 Thessalonians 1:8-9).

Question: *You want us to understand that the Word of the Lord proclaims the coming of the Lord in glory—His appearing, can you give Scripture for it?*

Yes. I will give three from the Apostolic preaching in the Acts of the Apostles. Peter said, "Repent. ... And He (God) shall send Jesus Christ, which before was preached unto you: whom the heaven must receive until the times of restitution of all things, which God hath spoken by the mouth of all His holy prophets since the world began" (Acts 3:19-21). Again, "And He commanded us to preach unto the people, and to testify that it is He which is ordained of God to be the Judge of the quick and dead" (chapter 10:42). Paul said, "God ... now commandeth all men everywhere to repent: because He hath appointed a day, in the which He will judge the world in righteousness by that Man whom He hath ordained; whereof He hath given assurance unto all men, in that He hath raised Him from the dead" (chapter 17:30-31).

THE JUDGMENT AND THE BLESSING AT HIS COMING

Question: *One of those Scriptures speaks of blessing, and the others of judgment; which is it that the appearing of the Lord will bring?*

God's purpose is the blessing of men, and Christ is coming for blessing and to fulfil the Scripture, "I have set Thee to be a light to the Gentiles, that Thou shouldest be for salvation unto the ends of the earth" (Isaiah 49:6; Acts 13:47), but judgment must go before the blessing, because of what men are. It is the persistent rebellion of men against God, that makes judgment a necessity. Yet judgment is God's strange work; He does not delight in it, He delights in mercy. This comes out in the very language that Scripture uses. When it is a question of judgment, we read "a *short work* will the Lord make upon the earth" (Romans 9:28), but when it is a *question of mercy*, "*He is longsuffering*, not willing that any should perish" (2 Peter 3:9). When vengeance is in view it is "the *day of vengeance*" (Isaiah 61:2), but when mercy, it is *"the acceptable year of the Lord"* (Luke 4:19). It is because God's terms of grace are rejected, and because the world will not obey the Gospel of our Lord Jesus Christ, and because men will not receive the knowledge of God when they may, that judgment must come, and it surely will come, though long delayed. The blessing will also come, "He shall come down like rain upon the mown grass" (Psalm 72:6). THE RAIN SPEAKS OF THE BLESSING, BUT "THE MOWN GRASS" MEANS THAT THE SCYTHE OF JUDGMENT WILL HAVE SWEPT THE FIELD BEFORE THE BLESSING DESCENDS.

Question: *But the Lord will not come in judgment as long as His Church is on the earth?*

No, because evil will not come into its full manifestation as long as the church is here, and God withholds His judgment until evil reaches its climax, that none may charge Him with unrighteousness. That is plain from 2 Thessalonians 2. The mystery of iniquity is already working, and those who are taught of God can discern it; indeed it is obtruding itself everywhere, in the increasing lawlessness, the impatience at authority, the disdain of God's claims and the diminishing of His fear in the world, the rejection of the great truths of the Word, the spread of ritualism and modernism, and the substitution of "Science falsely so called" for the Gospel in professed Christian circles; yet there is a restraining power here. There is that which withholdeth, or restraineth, and "He who now letteth (or hindereth), will let, until He be taken out of the way" (chapter 2:6-7). He that hindereth is the Holy Spirit of God who dwells in the church. As long as He is here it will be said to all the pride and purposes of men, "Hitherto shalt thou come and no further, and here shall all thy proud waves be stayed" (Job 38:11).

"The Man of Sin" and "That Wicked One"

We have often seen it, especially during the last quarter of a century, when evil forces have seemed to be rising up in irresistible waves, threatening to overwhelm all law and order, they have been checked and have subsided, and Christians have still been able to "pray for kings and for all that be in authority, that we may lead quiet and peaceable lives in all godliness and honesty" (1 Timothy 2:1-2). But when the church is completed and taken up to Heaven, the Holy Spirit will go with it, and God will allow men to have their own way. Then "that man of sin", "the son of perdition" (2 Thessalonians 2:3) and "that wicked one" (verse 8) will be revealed. In these two men—the Beast and the false prophet, who is also called Antichrist, and of whom we read in Revelation chapters 13, 17, 19,—Satan will find vessels of wrath, through whom he will work his will, and by them he will make his most desperate attempt to hold the world against God and Christ (see Revelation 16:13-14; 17:14). It is against these and their deluded followers, that the Lord will appear in judgment. Revelation 19:11-21 describes this appearing. Every name and character that He bears in that vivid description of His appearing is consistent with the event. He is the Faithful and the True, in contrast to the false pretensions of men and the lie with which the devil has deceived them (see 2 Thessalonians 2:9-11). "In righteousness He will judge and make war", against all "the deceivableness of unrighteousness in them that perish". He is called "the Word of God", for He will reveal God's holy wrath against *sin* in its completeness, as once He revealed His love to *sinners*. He is King of kings and Lord of lords, and will assert and establish His rights by the sharp sword of His mouth and with the rod of iron. There will be no mercy for those who oppose Him, for He will tread the winepress of the fierceness and wrath of Almighty God.

IN FLAMING FIRE

Question: *Does 2 Thessalonians 1, where we read of the Lord being revealed from heaven with His mighty angels in flaming fire, refer to the same time as Revelation 19?*

Yes, but in that passage the judgment takes a wider sweep, it has more than the armies of the Beast and false prophet in view. The flaming fire, which is figurative of judgment, is against all who know not God and obey not the Gospel of our Lord Jesus Christ. Those who have not obeyed the Gospel, are those who have heard it, and would apply to Christendom, and those who know not God are those who have had the opportunity of knowing Him, but who have not availed themselves of it. The judgment will fit the crimes and the conditions in which men are found; it will be a discriminating judgment, executed in absolute righteousness. Another passage that fits in with those already cited is Revelation 1:7, "Behold, He cometh with clouds, and every eye shall see Him, and they also which pierced Him: and all kindreds of the earth shall wail because of Him. Even so, Amen." That word plainly describes the Lord's appearing, not to any section of mankind, but to the whole world, and it is a parallel word to Matthew 24:30, where the Lord Himself says, "Then shall appear the sign of the Son of Man in Heaven: and then shall the tribes of the earth mourn, and they shall see the Son of Man coming in the clouds of Heaven with power and great glory." He comes thus to judge the living at His appearing, the dead will not come before Him until the great white Throne (Revelation 20), which judgment will take place after the close of His Millennial Kingdom.

The Gospel of the Kingdom

Who will enter into the blessing of the Millennial Kingdom at the Lord's Appearing?

Will there be a second chance for those who reject the Gospel of the grace of God?

How will the Lord appear to the waiting remnant?

"WAITING FOR THE COMING"

The Gospel of the Kingdom

Question: *There will be many who will enter into blessing under the reign of the Lord in the Millennium: if the judgment is to be world-wide, who will these be?*

They will be a remnant of Israel, and a great company of Gentiles, and as God's dealings with these two will be different, it will be well to consider them separately. For this the Lord's words in Matthew 24 will help us. Under the godless, devil-inspired domination of the Beast and Antichrist there "shall be great tribulation, such as was not since the beginning of the world to this time, no, nor ever shall be" (verse 21). These words are from the Lord's own lips, which fact gives them a special force. But in the midst of that tribulation which will beat more fiercely on the Jews than upon any other people, the Lord will have His elect, and for their sake the days will be shortened (verse 22). The elect of this verse will be found among the Jews, and in verse 31 there are others who are to be gathered together from the four winds, from one end of heaven to the other; these are probably not only Jews, that is, men of the tribe of Judah, but also of the whole of Israel. They are elect, which means the sovereign mercy of God has chosen them. But how will they be distinguished from the rest of the rebellious people? God's way has always been to bring such to light by a testimony from Himself, and the testimony then will be the Gospel of the Kingdom. "This Gospel of the Kingdom shall be preached in all the world for a witness unto all nations; and then shall the end come" (verse 14).

This Gospel will not be the Gospel of the grace of God, which tells of full redemption in Christ, and the sealing of the Holy Spirit and of heavenly hopes, which we have heard and believed; though it will be a Gospel of grace surely, and Christ will be the theme of it, or it would be no Gospel at all, but it will tell of the coming of the Lord as King, of His kingdom to be established on the earth as John the Baptist and the Lord Himself and His disciples proclaimed when He was here. It will be the proclamation of His supremacy over all, and the test will be, whether this Word of God and testimony of Jesus is received or rejected.

Those who receive the mark of the Beast in their foreheads and hands and worship his image, will not receive it, but those who refuse that delusion of the devil will; and by this testimony, not only the nation of the Jews, but all nations will be sharply divided. And as those who will be for the Beast and Antichrist will at that time be in the ascendancy, those who are for Christ will suffer great persecution. Many will be martyred, and have a heavenly reward, for they will have part in "the first resurrection" and shall "live and reign with Christ a thousand years" (Revelation 20:4-5). Others will be preserved and sustained by the Lord through the tribulation and will endure to the end, and they shall be saved for the Millennial Kingdom (Matthew 24:13). We must bear in mind that Matthew 24 has this time of tribulation in view and does not apply to the present time.

Will there be another chance for those who reject the Gospel?

Question: *Two questions arise in the mind from what you have said. 1st, Does it mean that there will be a second chance for those who reject the Gospel now and may be alive then? 2nd, Who will preach this Gospel of the Kingdom?*

There will certainly be no second opportunity for those who have refused God's salvation as it is now preached; "How shall we escape if we neglect so great salvation?" (Hebrews 2:3). The Gospel of the grace of God is God's best; if the best does not appeal to the heart of a man, nothing else will. But there are hundreds of millions in the world who have never heard the Gospel, and who know nothing of the Christian faith, except as some of them have seen it, so horribly corrupted as in Roman Catholic and Greek church lands. Pernicious books have been published in which it has been taught, that some who do not receive Christ as Saviour now, will refuse to yield to Antichrist and suffer martyrdom, but the Word says, "Because they received not the love of the truth, that they might be saved. And for this cause God shall send them strong delusion, that they should believe a lie: that they all might be damned who believed not the truth, but had pleasure in unrighteousness" (2 Thessalonians 2:10-12). That surely is conclusive, as are many other Scriptures.

As to who will proclaim this gospel, we learn from Revelation 11 that a new testimony to God will be given in Jerusalem by two witnesses, raised up and empowered by God, and though the majority will rejoice when they are slain, we may be sure that their witness will not be in vain. The Spirit of God will use it and the remnant will be born again. They will be "an afflicted and poor people and they shall trust in the Name of the LORD" (Zephaniah

3:12). The Lord's words to His apostles in Matthew 10 and Luke 21 will have a special reference to them, and they will go forth to speak with "a mouth of wisdom" that He will give them. In Matthew 25:40 the Lord speaks of them as "these My brethren". "The Lord gave the word: great was the company of those that published it" (Psalm 68:11).

The Elect Remnant

Question: *How will the Lord appear to this elect remnant?*

He will appear when the tribulation-persecution of the Jewish nation under the Antichrist will have reached its height, and His coming will bring it to an end. All nations will be gathered against Jerusalem and the city shall be taken, "then the LORD shall go forth and fight against those nations" (Zechariah 14). His appearing will be the destruction of those foes, but it will be the deliverance of the Godly Jews who are looking for Him. "To them that look for Him shall He appear … unto salvation" (Hebrews 9:28). "His feet shall stand in that day on the Mount of Olives … and the Mount of Olives shall cleave in the midst thereof toward the east and toward the west, and there shall be a very great valley … and ye shall flee to the valley of the mountains … and the LORD my God shall come and all the saints with Thee" (Zechariah 14:4-5). This passage throws light on the Lord's words in Matthew 24:15-16. "When ye therefore shall see the abomination of desolation, spoken of by Daniel the prophet, stand in the holy place (whoso readeth, let him understand). Then let them which be in Judea flee into the mountains." And it will be the fulfilment of Acts 1:11. "This same Jesus, which is taken up from you into Heaven, shall so come in like manner as ye have seen Him go into Heaven." He will return to the very spot from which He went up, His feet will stand again upon the mount of Olives.

As Joseph revealed himself to his guilty brethren of old (Genesis 45) and they confessed their sin of selling and persecuting him, so will the Lord reveal Himself to Israel who betrayed and sold Him into the hands of the Gentiles, and they will repent and mourn and confess. "The spirit of grace and supplications" shall be poured out upon them, and they shall look upon Him "whom they have pierced, and they shall mourn for Him as one mourneth for his only son, and is in bitterness for his firstborn" (Zechariah 12:10). "And they shall ask what are these wounds in Thine hands? Then He shall answer, Those with which I was wounded in the house of My friends" (Zechariah 13:6). It is thus that they will be brought to own the once crucified Jesus as their great Messiah. And it shall be said in that day of Him, "Lo, this is our God; we have waited for Him, and He will save us; this is the LORD: we have waited for Him, we will be glad and rejoice in His salvation" (Isaiah 25:9).

"WAITING FOR THE COMING"

The Word of God and the Coming of the Lord

Tampering with the Word.

The sign of the last days.

The Lord's last word to His church.

"WAITING FOR THE COMING"

The Word of God and the Coming of the Lord

We do not believe in making much of what may appear to be signs of the coming again of our Lord, for we may be so easily mistaken in these and injure souls by turning them to sensational and passing events rather than to Christ. Our business is to minister the truth as to the One who is coming, to so speak of Him and occupy the hearts of His saints with Himself, that they will long to see Him, and will cry, "Come, Lord Jesus." But there are some signs we cannot evade; they force themselves on our notice continually and shout at us wherever we turn. One of these is the way the Word of God is treated by many who have professed to have heard it, and to have become His servants as a result of it. How presumptuously they treat the Holy Word!

It is JESUS, our Lord, who, in this last chapter of the Revelation, declares Himself to be the Alpha and Omega, the first and the last, the beginning and the end, who testifies that every word of it is sacred, and not to be tampered with; and solemnly warns those that hear it of the terrible and eternal pains and penalties that those must suffer who dare either to add to it or take from it

(Revelation 22:13-19). But this solemn warning seems to have no weight, and the Lord Jesus Himself seems to have no authority with these men, who set their boasted learning above His Word, and think themselves competent to criticise it, and to say what of it is truth and what is error, what is the Word of God in it, and what the ecstatic dreams of a fallible man.

To those who are subject to the Lord and to His Word, and delighted to be so because of the joy and blessing that such subjection gives now, and the certainty and hope that it gives as to the future, "the words of the prophecy of this book" are infallible and sure, and so, indeed, are the words of all Scripture, and to them this profane and impious tampering with the words of Scripture is a sign of the last times, in which men are casting off the fear of God and despising His Word, and taking "counsel together against the LORD and against His Anointed, saying, Let us break their bands asunder, and cast away their cords from us" (Psalm 2:2-3).

It is by His Word that God holds and exercises the consciences of men, but if they refuse to accept the Word as the Word, and arrogate to themselves the right to choose and refuse those parts of it that suit their moods and whims, what hold has God upon them? They have in this cast away His cords from them and broken His bands asunder, and they imagine that they are free.

This is a sign of the last days, and with it the Lord connects His coming again: *"He who testifies these things saith, Surely, I come quickly"* (Revelation 22:20). Shall we not then, as we see His Word so mishandled, expect Him? When men will not have the Word of God, which is a word of grace and warning, to enlighten and correct and restrain and bless them, but will go their own wilful ways in defiance of His Word and will, is it not then the time for Him to appear who will judge the world in righteousness? And when those who by solemn oath have pledged themselves to be the faithful custodians of His Word are faithlessly treating it as a conglomeration of truth and fable, is it not the time for the Faithful and True Witness to appear? And since the time has come when they will not endure sound doctrine but, having itching ears, heap to themselves teachers, who deny that judgment is coming, and scoff at the thought of God's intervention in the affairs of the world (2 Timothy 4:3-4; 2 Peter 3:3-4), and are both adding to and taking from—chiefly taking from—the words of the prophecy of this book, is it not the time for Him to fulfil His word, and come quickly?

THE LAST WORD TO HIS CHURCH

It is His last word, and is it not as sure as any other word that He has spoken? Shall we accept every other word in this book as the Word of God and have a doubt about this? It is His last word, and it is a word from His heart for the heart of His church, His bride, and it is the heart that will understand it and not the head. He had said unto John of the whole book, "These sayings are faithful and true; and the Lord God of the holy prophets sent His angel to show unto His servants the things that must shortly be done. Behold I come quickly: blessed is he that keepeth the sayings of the prophecy of this book" (Revelation 22:6-7); and will not he be blessed who keeps this saying, and treasures it as the last word of the Heavenly Bridegroom, the bright Morning Star? And what will the response be from the heart that treasures this saying? There can be but one. "Amen; come, Lord Jesus."

It is His last word in this book in which we hear the thunders of heavenly praise; in which we see the pride and crimes of men challenge the very supremacy of God and call aloud for the wrath that is revealed from heaven against all unrighteousness, and which shall crush them utterly; in which the Lamb girds on His victorious sword and triumphs over all His foes, for He is King of kings and Lord of lords; and in His last words in this book the voice of judgment changes to words of love; the voice that makes the earth tremble now speaks in tender tones to the hearts of His saints, that in them there might be awakened a response to His desire, and that that response might find expression in a cry that will be as sweetest music to Him, "Come, Lord Jesus." He has heard this cry from many lips.

"They tasted His love and their souls were on fire,
While they waited in patience His face to behold."
(Thomas Kelly, 1769-1854)

Is not this the time when He should hear it afresh? Nothing short of His coming, His presence, can satisfy the hearts of those who know that they are loved by Him. And His coming is drawing nigh. It ever was nigh to His heart; we shall show how near it is to ours by going forth to meet Him with this cry upon our lips.

Let all who love the Lord remember that He cannot come to put the world right and establish God's righteousness in the earth, until He has taken His church, His bride, out of it. We can hasten that glorious day for which all creation groans, by looking earnestly for Him and crying with hearts expectant and fervent, "Come, Lord Jesus."

Events to Take Place on Earth Between the Rapture and the Eternal State

The seven seals.

The seven trumpets.

Satan cast out of Heaven.

The Great Tribulation.

Armageddon.

The judgment of the living nations.

Peace and blessing.

End of the thousand years.

The Great White Throne.

Eternity.

"WAITING FOR THE COMING"

Events to Take Place on Earth Between the Rapture and the Eternal State

The great event which forms the hope of every true believer on the Lord Jesus Christ is His coming into the air to raise the dead and change the living and translate them to His Father's house in heaven. No event is foretold with greater clearness and precision than this, as we have already seen from 1 Corinthians 15:52; 1 Thessalonians 4:15-17; John 14:1-3; Philippians 3:20-21.

Though all who have died in faith since Abel's day will be raised in glory at this time, for they all belong to Christ, yet this event has the Church specially in view. It will include all who have believed in Him for the salvation of their souls from Pentecost. He has redeemed the church by His own blood, and He is coming for it and will present it to Himself, a glorious Church, not having spot or wrinkle or any such thing (Ephesians 5:27). "Behold the Bridegroom."

The Church having been caught up to Heaven, the saints will pass in review before the judgment seat of Christ and the marriage of the Lamb will take place. And God begins to move specially with regard to the earth. This brings us to Revelation 4, where God appears as the eternal and self-existing One who has created all things for His own pleasure, and who is about to assert His rights which have been denied by men upon the earth, and to reconcile all things in heaven and on earth to Himself, that He might find His pleasure in them. In Revelation 5 the Lord appears as the Lion of the tribe of Juda, who, having been slain as the sacrificial Lamb, alone is worthy and able to establish God's will upon the earth in power. He takes the seven-sealed scroll of judgment from the hand of God to open the seals of it, and to execute the judgments therein written, for only by judgment can way be made for His kingdom to come.

THE OPENING OF THE SEALS

Anarchy, with the attendant sufferings, misery, slaughter, famine, and pestilence, follows *the opening of the seals* (chapter 6), in, we judge, the professedly Christian lands, for they speak of the Lamb (verse 16), a title by which the Lord is known only where the Gospel has been preached. This condition of things is not due to the direct judgment of God, but seems to be the outcome of the unrestrained development of the pretentious and promising schemes by men for their own betterment apart from God. Their wisdom turns out to be folly, and the way that seemeth right unto them ends in death (Proverbs 16:25). This condition of things will open the way for the rise of the Beast—the devil-inspired empire and its ruthless head (Revelation 13).

There first appears:

A rider on a white horse, with bow and crown, going forth conquering and to conquer. The victories gained are bloodless, and tell in striking symbol of some great policy or movement that will promise peace, prosperity, and goodwill, and fill the hearts of men with hope and self-congratulation. These hopes are speedily dashed to the ground, for the white horse and his rider are followed by

A rider on a red horse, who takes peace from the earth, so that they kill one another; and this seems to indicate internecine strife rather than war between nations; it will be a class warfare in which Communism will play its devilish part; for men, having given up God and His laws entirely, will each hate his neighbour as he loves himself.

A rider on a black horse follows, telling of grim famine, crushing with its miseries those who escape the sword, and making the way easy for

A rider on a pale horse, who will come forth killing with sword, with hunger, and with death, and with the beasts of the earth. And this is not the end as some men fondly hope that death must be the end of all things for them, for

Hell follows with him to claim the souls of those whose bodies are slain by the overwhelming calamities that the prophet sees. How quick, how terrible is THIS DESCENT OF MAN *from the promise of the rider on the white horse to the hopeless depths of hell*. Such will be the descent of man when God's preserving mercy is withdrawn from him. Even now the swift steeds are bound to the chariot and are straining at the curb, and would take that steep gradient at a headlong gallop, but for the restraining hand of God. Meanwhile men, so blind are they, would fondly believe that they were speeding to the attainment of their most cherished ambitions. The ascent of man is a false dream, a delusion of the old serpent; the descent of man is a terrible fact. The only hope of deliverance from sin and Satan's power, and death and hell is in and through Christ. *Blessed are all they that put their trust in Him* (Psalm 2:12).

The Seven Trumpets

The Fall of a Great Maritime Power, and the destruction of that which seems prosperous on the earth, is indicated under *the Trumpets*, by the burning up of a third part of the trees and grass, and a great mountain being cast into the sea destroying a third part of the ships that are in it (Revelation 8) in the same sphere as that affected by the seals; but the awful calamities seem to spread to heathen lands in chapter 9, as indicated by the fact that idolatry comes into the catalogue of crimes in verse 20. We see in these visions a world that has refused God and His Christ at the mercy of men's passions and the malice of demons. Especially under the sounding of the trumpets men seem to be left to the miseries that the devil and his emissaries from hell can inflict upon them.

Palestine Peopled with Jews

At this time the Jews will be fully established in Palestine under the protection of a maritime nation (Isaiah 18). Their temple will be restored to them in Jerusalem, but they will still refuse God's testimony and will rejoice when His witnesses are slain (Revelation 11).

Satan cast out of Heaven

The seat of spiritual authority that lies behind all great movements in the world is in the heavens. Satan occupies this position now (Ephesians 2:2; 6:12), though God is above all and only permits evil to go so far. But he is to be cast out of this place by Michael the archangel (Revelation 12) to make way for the Church, which is the Lamb's bride, the holy Jerusalem, for it must eventually have that place for the blessing of the world (Revelation 21:9-27), and to prepare the way also for the Lord's kingdom on earth which will have Jerusalem and Israel as its centre.

Michael is the great spiritual prince that stands for Israel (Daniel 10:21; 12:1).

THE RISE OF THE BEAST

Being cast out of heaven Satan exercises all his power and ingenuity in the reconstruction of the Roman Empire. It comes up out of the anarchy of Revelation 6, and to its head, the Beast-Satan, the Dragon, gives his power and his seat (Revelation 13), and his authority (verse 2). In this person military dictatorship, godless, blasphemous, diabolical, and ruthless will come to its full power; he will devour and break in pieces, and all those who dare to resist his political schemes—the residue—he will stamp beneath his feet (Daniel 7:7).

The intention of Satan in this, his masterpiece, is to hold the kingdoms of the world against the Lord and His Christ, and the ten kingdoms that form the Roman Empire will join in this, and give their power to the Beast in order to make war with the Lamb who is Lord of lords and King of kings (Revelation 17:12-14).

ANTICHRIST WILL ALSO ARISE –

as the great coadjutor of the Beast. He will be an apostate Jew, regarding not the God of his fathers (Daniel 11:37), and will be the leader of the Jews in Jerusalem. The Dragon (Satan), the Beast, and the False Prophet (Antichrist) will form a trinity of evil (Revelation 16:13).

THE LAST WEEK OF DANIEL'S SEVENTY COMMENCES

The Prince of the same people, the Romans, who destroyed the temple and city of Jerusalem, *i.e.*, the Beast, will make a covenant with the leaders of the Jews for one week, a week of years, or seven years; this is the last week of the seventy of Daniel's prophecy that still waits to be fulfilled (Daniel 9:20-27). This covenant is referred to in

Isaiah 28:14-20 as being on the part of the leaders of the Jews a God-defying covenant. They will at this time believe that they are at last firmly established in their land, and that an era of peace without God has been inaugurated. They will say, "Peace, and there is no peace." They will build a wall of protection about themselves, and daub it with untempered mortar, but a stormy wind will rend it, and great hailstones shall consume it in the wrath of God (Ezekiel 13:10-15).

The Great Tribulation

In the midst of the week the Beast will treat his covenant with the Jews as "a scrap of paper", to be scorned and torn according to his imperious will. The great tribulation will then begin, which will spend its greatest fury upon the Jews (Jeremiah 30:7; Daniel 12:1; Matthew 24:8), but which will also try all that dwell upon the earth (Revelation 3:10). During this period all will be compelled to receive the mark of the Beast and worship him, or suffer boycott and death (Revelation 13:16-17). A remnant will be preserved by the power of God (Revelation 12:14, 16). The Church will not be on earth but in heaven during this period of greatest distress, for she is to be saved out of the hour of it (Revelation 3:10).

The Remnant and their Service

At this time there will appear the two witnesses for God at Jerusalem, in the power of Elias (Revelation 11), and the remnant which keep the commandments of God and have the testimony of Jesus (Revelation 12:17). To these Matthew 24, Mark 13, and Luke 21:8-19, 25-33 will apply. The commission given to the apostles in Matthew 10 will be taken up again, and the sufferings and persecutions and martyrdoms there promised will be endured, and by this remnant a people will be prepared amongst the Jews to receive the Lord at His coming, and "they shall not have gone over the cities of Israel till the Son of man be come" (verse 23). Others will go further afield and preach "this Gospel of the Kingdom" "in all the world for witness unto all nations" (Matthew 24:14).

BABYLON THE GREAT, THE CORRUPT CHURCH OF ROME, OVERTHROWN

After the translation of the true Church to heaven, the false profession in Christendom will all be merged into the Romish Church, and this will become more powerful and greater than ever in the past, and as the scarlet woman, corrupt, blood-drunken, and splendid, she will ride upon the Beast, the political and military power, but she is to be destroyed by it as described in Revelation 17 and 18.

THE GREAT APOSTASY

Then there will be no semblance of *public* religion in Christendom or in Jewry (for the Jewish sacrifice will be stopped by the law of the Beast, Daniel 9:27), except the worship of the Beast himself, the exaltation of man above all that is called God. Then the great apostasy will have come to its head (2 Thessalonians 2:3-12), and the abomination of desolation will be set up in the Temple at Jerusalem, probably an image of the Beast (Daniel 9:27; Matthew 24:15). At this sign those who are faithful to God amongst the Jews in Judea will flee to the mountains (Matthew 24:16).

This complete apostasy from God will make men ready to fight against Him, and the

INVASIONS OF PALESTINE WILL TAKE PLACE.

Towards the end of the second half of Daniel's last week the *King of the South* (Egypt) will invade Palestine, in order to attack Antichrist (the wilful king) at Jerusalem. Simultaneously the *King of the North* will sweep down upon the land and attack the armies from the south and overthrow them and compel the whole force from the south to submit to his will and support his campaign against Jerusalem (Daniel 11:40-45). The King of the North is the Assyrian of Old Testament prophecy, the overflowing scourge (Isaiah 28:15).

The Gathering of the Kings for Armageddon

Revelation 16:13-16 describes how the kings of the whole earth and of the world will be gathered into Palestine at this time, and Joel 3:9-11 foretells that war will be the supreme business of all nations. "They will beat their ploughshares into swords and their pruning hooks into spears." Various political reasons will doubtless move these kings to march upon the Holy Land, but the object of Satan, who will move behind the scenes so as to involve all in this crisis, is to fight against the Lamb and hold Jerusalem and the Holy Land against Him. But God will turn all to His own glory. So that in reality God will gather them there (Zechariah 14:2), and will stain the pride of all militarism and glory of men, and smash it for ever outside the city which He has chosen to place His name there. The *kings of the East*, probably four, with an almost countless host, will also gather there (Revelation 9:13-19; 16:12).

The four angels that are to be loosed beyond Euphrates, seem to represent four great nations, in the east, and that river is to be dried up to make the way of these kings and their vast armies easy. This is probably the true "yellow peril", and the invasion of Europe the purpose. It may be that the armies of Europe under the Beast march into Palestine to withstand them. Anyhow these multitudes will be gathered in the valley of Jehoshaphat (Joel 3), not to destroy one another, but to be judged by the Lord.

THE COMING OF THE KING OF KINGS AND LORD OF LORDS

The sudden appearance of the Lord in this character has special reference to the Beast and false prophet and their armies, for the Beast will have assumed this place and title, which is the Lord's alone. These two devil-inspired leaders of men are cast into the lake of fire, and their armies are destroyed by the word of the Lord (Revelation 19:11-21).

IN FLAMING FIRE TAKING VENGEANCE

Simultaneously all who had not obeyed the Gospel of our Lord Jesus Christ, which they must have heard to be judged on this ground, whether with the armies of the Beast or not, will be destroyed at the glorious appearing of the Lord (2 Thessalonians 1:7-9).

HIS FEET SHALL STAND UPON MOUNT OLIVET

He shall appear for the salvation of the godly remnant of Israel who look for Him (Hebrews 9:28), and who have fled to the mountains according to His Word (Matthew 24:16). In the same manner as, and from the same spot from whence He went up He shall return (Acts 1:11; Zechariah 14:4). And then the Lord will sit to judge the heathen round about (Zechariah 14; Joel 3:12-16).

ISRAEL DELIVERED AND THE KINGDOM ESTABLISHED

Those of the Jewish nation who have been faithful to Him during the great tribulation now brought to an end by the coming of the Lord will have a special place in His Kingdom, but He will gather His elect, not of the Jews only, but of the ten tribes also from north, south, east, and west (Matthew 24:31), and all Israel shall be saved

(Romans 11:26). The nation born again, and with the law written in their hearts, shall live unto God (Ezekiel 37).

THE INVASION OF THE LAND BY GOG AND MAGOG

This invasion of a mighty host from Russia and adjacent lands foretold in Ezekiel 38, 39, after the striking description of the restoration of Israel in chapter 37, appears to take place after Israel has accepted their Messiah, and when they "are at rest and dwell safely" (chapter 38:11). The destruction of these armies is described in chapter 39.

THE JUDGMENT OF THE LIVING NATIONS

The last section of mankind still alive on the earth to be judged of the Lord are those that have been farthest off from Him, morally and spiritually, and who have had the least knowledge of His will, the heathen nations. This judgment is described by the Lord in Matthew 25:31-46. It is not as the Messiah of Israel that He judges these nations, but as Son of man, who is set over all things, and it takes place when He sits upon the throne of His glory in that character. The test for all who stand before Him then and there will be how they have treated His brethren (verse 40), who had preached to the ends of the earth *"this Gospel of the Kingdom"*, who had been the heralds of His kingdom.

PEACE AND BLESSING –

will follow which shall be earth-wide, having its centre on earth in Jerusalem (Isaiah 2:2-5). But all the light and wisdom and blessing will come through the heavenly Jerusalem, which is the wife of the Lamb, His helpmeet in the place of administration that is given to Him (Revelation 21:24). This will be the Millennial age of which the Old Testament prophets spoke in glowing words, and in it will be made manifest to all the glory that is to follow upon the sufferings of Christ (1 Peter 1:11).

PRINCIPALITIES AND POWERS AND DOMINIONS –

other than those connected with the earth will have to be subdued by Him, and these vast spiritual dominions will by His power be reconciled to God (Colossians 1:20), for *"He must reign*, till He hath put all enemies under His feet. The last enemy that shall be destroyed is death ... and when all things shall be subdued unto Him, then shall the Son also Himself be subject unto Him that put all things under Him, that God may be all in all" (1 Corinthians 15:25-28).

THE CLOSE OF THE THOUSAND YEARS –

reveals the fact that millions who had been born during their peaceful course had not been born again, and that they will be in heart and character just what man has ever been since the fall, ready to rebel against God; which they do with great enthusiasm when Satan, who had been chained up in the bottomless pit during the Millennium, is released for a little season (Revelation 20:7-9). The devil is then sent to his eternal doom, the lake of fire (verse 10).

THE GREAT WHITE THRONE

This will be the last judgment, the judgment of the dead who have died in their sins, all who stand there have but one judgment; they are shut off from the God whose mercy they had refused, and cast into the lake of fire, where the devil is whom they had served (Revelation 20:11-15).

THE ETERNAL STATE

The earth and the heaven having fled away from the face of the Judge upon the throne, a new heaven and a new earth come into being, and the "tabernacle of God is with men, and He shall dwell with them, and they shall be His people, and God Himself shall be with them, and be their God. And God shall wipe away all tears from their eyes; and there shall be no more death, neither sorrow nor crying, neither shall there be any more pain; for the former things are passed away. And He that sat upon the throne said, Behold, I make all things new. And He said unto me, Write: for these things are true and faithful. And He said unto me, It is done. I am Alpha and Omega, the beginning and the end. I will give unto him that is athirst of the fountain of the water of life freely" (Revelation 21:3-6).

Anticipation

I read in the infallible Scriptures
  Of a day that is yet to be,
When the glory and power of Jesus,
  Men, angels and devils shall see;
His name above all names exalted,
  All knees in His presence shall bend,
And tongues without number confess Him,
  His praises as incense ascend.

Oh, sing ye, and publish the story;
  Rejoice, for Jehovah doth reign;
Give honour, dominion and glory,
  To God and the Lamb that was slain.

All eyes in the glory shall see Him,
  The Lamb in the midst of the throne;
And thousands on thousands shall own Him
  Worthy of the kingdom and crown.
For He hath prevailed, and He only,
  To open the book of God's will,
Undo all the works of the devil,
  And earth with God's righteousness fill.

"WAITING FOR THE COMING"

All angels shall say, Alleluia!
  All heaven shall add its Amen;
Let us shout and be glad and give honour
  To Him who for sinners was slain.
For His wife hath made herself ready,
  The long-looked-for marriage has come,
And heaven doth ring with His praises,
  His foes at His footstool are dumb.

His kingdom shall come, and the prayers
  Of His saints be answered at last,
And justice and mercy shall flourish,
  Toil, grief and oppression be past.
His sceptre stretched out for the needy,
  He'll feed all the poor with His bread;
And over all realms in His kingdom
  Contentment and peace shall be spread.

J. T. Mawson

Tune: The Great Judgment Morning.

Awakening Songs. Pickering & Inglis.

"WAITING FOR THE COMING"

The coming again of the Lord Jesus, and consequent events, from other standpoints, is dealt with in the books *"For This Cause"* and *"Jerusalem"* by the same author.

OTHER BOOKS FROM SCRIPTURE TRUTH PUBLICATIONS
Understanding the Old Testament series:

How to Overcome by John T Mawson
  ISBN 978-0-901860-62-0 (paperback)
  144 pages; April 2009

Delivering Grace by John T Mawson
  ISBN 978-0-901860-64-4 (paperback)
  ISBN 978-0-901860-78-1 (hardback)
  192 pages; March 2007

The Tabernacle's Typical Teaching by A J Pollock
  ISBN 978-0-901860-65-1 (paperback)
  236 pages; July 2009

Psalm 119: A Commentary on the Entire Psalm by Cor Bruins
  ISBN 978-0-901860-88-0 (paperback)
  186 pages; March 2010

Elijah: A Prophet of the Lord by Hamilton Smith
  ISBN 978-0-901860-68-2 (paperback)
  80 pages; March 2007

Elisha: The Man of God by Hamilton Smith
  ISBN 978-0-901860-79-8 (paperback)
  92 pages; March 2007

The Gospel in Job by Yannick Ford
  ISBN 978-0-901860-76-7 (paperback)
  ISBN 978-0-901860-77-4 (hardback)
  112 pages; March 2007

Lessons from Ezra by Ted Murray
  ISBN 978-0-901860-75-0 (paperback)
  84 pages; March 2007

"WAITING FOR THE COMING"

Lessons from Nehemiah by Ted Murray
ISBN 978-0-901860-86-6 (paperback)
124 pages; August 2008

Understanding Christianity series:

Seek Ye First by John S Blackburn
ISBN 978-0-901860-61-3 (paperback)
ISBN 978-0-901860-02-6 (hardback)
136 pages; February 2007

God and Relationships by Cor Bruins
ISBN 978-0-901860-36-1 (paperback)
108 pages; August 2006

"The Epistle of Christ" edited by F. B. Hole
ISBN 978-0-901860-73-6 (paperback)
140 pages; March 2008

"Comforted of God" complied by Algernon J Pollock
ISBN 978-0-901860-63-7 (paperback)
110 pages; April 2010

Short Papers on the Church by Hamilton Smith
ISBN 978-0-901860-80-4 (paperback)
96 pages; March 2008

God's Inspiration of the Scriptures by William Kelly
ISBN 978-0-901860-51-4 (paperback)
ISBN 978-0-901860-56-9 (hardback)
484 pages; March 2007

Lectures on the Church of God by William Kelly
ISBN 978-0-901860-50-7 (paperback)
244 pages; February 2007
ISBN 978-0-901860-55-2 (hardback)
244 pages; March 2007

www.ingramcontent.com/pod-product-compliance
Lightning Source LLC
Chambersburg PA
CBHW020009050426
42450CB00005B/381